When
Free Men
Shall Stand

When Free Men Shall Stand

U.S. Senator
JESSE HELMS

ZONDERVAN
PUBLISHING HOUSE
OF THE ZONDERVAN CORPORATION
GRAND RAPIDS, MICHIGAN 49506

Eighth printing   June 1978

Library of Congress Catalog Card Number 76-44609
ISBN 0-310-26009-7

Printed in the United States of America

In Gratitude

To my wife, a lady of unfailing patience and unyielding principles; to Mrs. Mary Grace Lucier and Mrs. Arlene Compton, for their tireless assistance in the technical preparation of this manuscript; and to Mr. A. J. Fletcher and Tom Ellis for being my faithful friends.

Oh, thus be it ever when free men shall stand
Between their loved homes and the war's desolation;
Blest with vict'ry and peace, may the Heav'n-rescued land
Praise the Pow'r that made and preserved us a nation!
Then conquer we must, when our cause it is just;
And this be our motto: "In God is our trust!"

From "The Star Spangled Banner"
by Francis Scott Key

If my people, which are called by my name, shall humble themselves, and pray, and seek my face, and turn from their wicked ways; then will I hear from heaven, and will forgive their sin, and will heal their land.

2 Chronicles 7:14

Man is not made for the State,
but the State for man.

Thomas Jefferson

Contents

Preface

PERHAPS IT is because I was born and reared in a small town that I have never been able to drive past the magnificent structure known as the U.S. Capitol without feeling a sense of pride in our country and a renewed gratitude for America's great heritage of freedom — a freedom which, with each passing day, I become more firmly convinced simply had to be a very special blessing from God.

I grew up in Monroe, the seat of Union County, North Carolina. That makes me, as an indulgent friend put it, a "country boy." Whatever I am, I am thankful for my parents and my teachers who left no doubt that being an American in the twentieth century is the greatest fortune that can befall a human being.

In the years since then, my career has enabled me to associate with the highest officials of our land. I have visited with dignitaries in many other countries having almost every variety of political arrangement. I have dined at the White House; I have seen presidents come and go. In a sense, I have been an eyewitness to history, and there have been countless times when I could scarcely believe I was there!

Still, for me, there is no sight in the world more stirring than that majestic white dome, brilliantly illuminated against the evening sky. Many are the times, especially after a tumultuous day in the Senate, when I have made it a point to pause and admire this great edifice and hope for another day's inspiration to do my small part to uphold the republic for which it stands. Though we have passed through some dark days in this city — and darker days may still await us — this spectacle crowning Capitol Hill has never disappointed me. Our Capitol is still the great shining beacon of freedom in the world.

Growing up in Monroe between the two world wars was an experience I would not trade for any material thing. From the perspective of years, I can look back and see that my contemporaries and I were able to absorb from our homes and our Southern environment great ideals — and few illusions.

My father served as the chief of the combined fire and police departments in Monroe. A man of solid worth and dignity, he was well-known and highly respected in the community. Our home ties were very strong, and the church the dominant influence in our lives. Small towns in the South, moreover, have seldom been known as havens of affluence, and the Great Depression hit them with a particular virulence.

These were times when our faith in God and in our country's institutions were put to a severe test. On the whole, we kept the faith and surmounted adversity. In the process, life was not without its rewards. The sense of community, compassion, resourcefulness, courage, pride, and self-reliance we knew then seems conspicuously absent from many luxurious subdivisions today.

No one will deny that, for comfort and convenience, American life today is a far cry from what it was in the thirties. And yet, in all my reading and reflection over the years, I never detected in the days of the depression the kind of spiritual desolation and cynicism, nor the urge toward violent revolution, that has gripped our country in the recent past. Characteristically Americans have always been a buoyant, optimistic people, and so this change in outlook seems all the more ominous.

There is a constant theme in the many letters I receive from people all over the country. They ask: What has happened to our moral fiber? Where have we lost the way? And above all, why is freedom in retreat all over the world?

Our political problems are nothing but our psychological and moral problems writ large. There is a great crisis of the spirit, a weariness of soul that has gradually paralyzed much of the Christian West. As a result, communism has taken over almost half of the world's population in our own lifetimes with little serious opposition.

For nearly two thousand years the Christian religion has warned us that the greatest sins we can fall into are presumption and despair. Because I believe this, I feel a duty to reiterate, however inadequately and unworthily, the great moral and political truths that have sustained us as an independent nation for two centuries — truths which, in our current climate of apathy and skepticism, are so gravely endangered.

A famous writer once said of Christianity that it had not been tried and found wanting; rather, it had been found difficult, and left untried. He was right, of course. And I believe a similar statement could be made about the philosophy of government which I myself have tried to espouse and which today is known as "conservatism."

For forty years an unending barrage of "deals" — the New Deal, the Fair Deal, the New Frontier, and the Great Society, not to mention court decisions tending in the same direction — have regimented our people and our economy and federalized almost every human enterprise. This onslaught has installed a gigantic scheme for redistributing the wealth that rewards the indolent and penalizes the hard-working.

We have bought every nostrum the liberals have been so insistent to sell us, and we have abandoned the sure prescription for freedom, for prosperity, and for survival that is the very genius of the Declaration of Independence and the Constitution.

I believe we can halt the long decline. There is nothing inevitable about it. There is a way back. And to whatever extent I can point out the signposts on that road, I offer the following chapters to my countrymen willing to join in this great undertaking.

When
Free Men
Shall Stand

CHAPTER ONE

The Spiritual Rebirth of Our Nation

THE SITUATION in our country today is remarkably similar to that in Israel in the days of the Judges when, Scripture tells us, "there arose another generation . . . who did not know the Lord or the work which he had done for Israel.

"And the people of Israel did what was evil in the sight of the Lord and served the Baals; and they forsook the Lord, the God of their fathers, who had brought them out of the land of Egypt; they went after other gods, from among the gods of the peoples who were round about them, and bowed down to them; and they provoked the Lord to anger" (Judges 2:10-12).

Spiritually we know we are all Israel, for Christ teaches that God's admonitions and promises to Israel will be fulfilled also in New Testament times and peoples. In the brief history of our own country since we gained our independence, we can look back upon a tremendous heritage of political freedom founded upon a biblical faith and a biblical understanding of the nature of man. Moreover, we can look back upon the material signs of God's blessing in a fruitful and bounteous country, with success in almost every enterprise in war and peace.

But within my own lifetime, I have seen the most ferocious assaults on Christian faith and morals; first on the part of the intellectual community, and then on the

15

part of the Government. Especially in the last twenty-five years, the federal government has not even tried to conceal its hostility to religion; now, with many of our churches in disarray, the attack is being prepared against the family as the last bastion opposing the totalitarian state.

Militant atheists and socialists have gone very far in imposing their view of life and man on almost every American institution. Atheism and socialism — or liberalism, which tends in the same direction — are inseparable entities: when you have men who no longer believe that God is in charge of human affairs, you have men attempting to take the place of God by means of the Superstate. The all-provident Government, which these liberals constantly invoke, is the modern-day version of Baal.

And what have we reaped as a nation from our many personal and collective delinquencies? Atheistic schools, rampaging crime, Godforsaken homes, drugs, abortion, pornography, permissiveness, and a sense of cynicism and spiritual desolation absolutely unprecedented in our country's history.

The Israelites in their time also opted for the New Morality. They were as enthusiastic as many of our contemporary thinkers about situation ethics, for we read, "In those days, there was no king in Israel; every man did what was right in his own eyes" (Judges 17:6).

Today even many people who consider themselves Christians are apt to identify the concept of freedom in social and political matters with some kind of autonomy that is exempt from obedience to God's law. They are eager not to be accused of "imperialism" or "superpatriotism" or adhering to outmoded standards of "middle-class morality." Even politicians are using a veneer of Christianity to cast discredit on the historic values and mission of the United States that have always been profoundly Christian.

It is debatable at just what point the United States

began to drift away from its Christian heritage. But I think we reached that point when many Americans turned away from the idea of salvation through Christ to that of salvation through technology or science or material affluence or the welfare state. When all these turned out to be dead ends, Americans began to seek escape, and the purveyors of drugs and pornography and vicarious violence were there to meet the need. Human nature left to its own devices has always been a wretched failure at explaining the meaning and destiny of life. This life, we know, is only a prelude to our eternal destiny; we can never be at peace when we ignore the spiritual and moral dimension of our earthly existence.

I have often meditated upon why God chose the time and place He did for His Son to be born into the world. In the long preparation for the coming of Christ, the world had seen the tremendous achievements of many civilizations. But neither the intellectual brilliance of the Greeks; nor the sober morals of the ancient Romans; nor the technological and organizational genius of the later Romans were enough to still the discontent of human hearts. God chose an obscure outpost of a decadent empire as the birthplace of His Son, and upon all the debris of human pride and presumption there came forth the anointed Savior. From that day to this, there has been only one Light of the World, one Hope of Mankind.

All through His earthly life, this Person took pains to point out that He was not in any way a political messiah. Quite the reverse holds true in Washington today, where many politicians and many factions contend relentlessly for the honor of being the very political messiah who will solve all our problems if only we give them more money and more power.

By and large, our people look in the wrong direction for their deliverance. We need to pay less attention to TV and newspaper commentaries and more to the "platforms" written by Matthew, Mark, Luke, and John. As Christians we need to work with missionary zeal to reinstate the rule of Christ in our sadly demoralized country.

We certainly need to pray more. We need to revive the respect for God's law that has been obliterated in individual consciences and in the nation's statutes.

As the Israelites learned time and again from the lash of their enemies, it was only by repentance and submission to the God of their Fathers that they could survive and prosper. Who can fail to see the chastisement of the human race in the long shadows of the Gulag Archipelago — shadows that are moving rapidly westward? As we learned to our astonishment in Vietnam, it is not by any combination of money and power and armaments that communism will be restrained, but only through faith in God, heroic discipline, and moral courage.

I pray every day for a rebirth of the spiritual values that made us a nation in the first place. If the Spirit of God were to rouse two hundred million Americans to action, there is no describing the greatness and glory in store for this country, or the blessings forthcoming to nations now held captive — if and when, once again, the United States rededicates itself to the cause of freedom under God's law.

CHAPTER TWO

The Roots of Freedom

MANY AMERICANS are content to believe that the freedoms they have traditionally enjoyed, and have come to accept as the order of nature, were initiated by the Declaration of Independence in 1776 and reaffirmed in the Bill of Rights in 1791. But the truth is that the War for Independence was only one short skirmish in a struggle whose origins go back into the mists of history.

Ultimately, the author of human liberty is almighty God, who endows each human being with free will. Every human being since Adam has been free to obey the laws of God, or to disobey them; to enjoy, in the words of Scripture, the glorious liberty of the sons of God, or to submit to his own slavery in sin. God Himself does not constrain our wills; in His infinite majesty, He respects the choices made by men.

At various times over thousands of years, the human race has attempted in faltering ways to set up for themselves governments that would respect the sense of freedom which, however dimly, each individual perceives in himself.

Very few nations in all recorded history ever achieved this goal. We see starts in this direction among the early Greeks and early Romans, but these were soon extinguished. It is a sobering fact that the freedom which has been the possession of Americans for two centuries has been a unique achievement. Only a small fraction of one percent of humanity has ever enjoyed the benefits of American citizenship and the liberties that it confers.

By far, the overwhelming majority of human beings who have lived on this earth have done so as the captives or the subjects or the slaves of somebody else. This is still true at this hour. Our indebtedness for the freedom Americans enjoy today spans many millennia. Remarkably enough, our debt is not to the great empires of ancient history, the Syrians or the Egyptians or the Romans who made civilization a reality, but to several tribes of wanderers who lived along the fringes of great empires and kept alive their identity and independence against the superstates of their day.

I refer first of all to the Jews, who preserved the exalted concept of the one God and the moral code He laid down for the human race, and who prepared the way for the true Liberator of mankind, Jesus Christ. From them we received the ethical foundation of our liberty.

For the genesis of our political institutions we must look to a region on the remotest fringe of the gigantic Roman Empire, to a region now known as the German province of Schleswig-Holstein. Here along the banks of the rivers that poured into the North Sea lived a collection of primitive tribes: the Angles, Saxons, and Jutes, who practiced a form of self-government. Even though Roman law was among the greatest achievements of human society, it is from these rude barbarians, rather than from the Romans, that we gained the all-important concept of limited government and the germ of those institutions that made delegated power possible and workable.

About the time the Roman Empire was collapsing before waves and waves of barbarian invaders, bands of Angles, Saxons, and Jutes were slowly emigrating from their homelands to the inviting meads of Britain that lay across the sea. With them went their ancient traditions of folk assemblies and local government.

They who subjugated the native Britons were themselves laid low in succeeding centuries by the Vikings and then, most devastatingly, by the Normans, who imposed the strict hierarchy of the feudal system on the England of the eleventh century. This system supplanted the earlier freeholdings almost without exception.

All across England, the tenants of the land quickly accepted the overlordship of the conquering nobles. The nobles held land from the king in return for military service. They subdued their fractious tenants and their rebellious neighbors and provided the security and stability that allowed the activities of daily life to continue unhindered.

Though many generations would go by under such conditions, the English never completely lost the impulse for self-government. Gradually the unending taxes, tolls, and other exactions to which they were subject taught them what their progeny centuries hence would discover in colonial America: security can sometimes be provided at too high a price, and what they needed most was relief from all this "protection." And so the stage was set for Magna Carta and the acceptance of traditional practices that are the very substance of English common law. Through trial and error, through the accumulated experience of centuries of Christian teaching, the English expressed their native genius in the institutions which, in the ensuing ages, would make personal freedom a practical ideal and would curb the power of the all-powerful state.

The great truth to be noted in this is the gradual evolution of personal rights and responsibilities in a nation whose instincts and experience led in this direction. Liberty in any form is not guaranteed by edicts or proclamations or slogans from the mob, but by order and discipline and a fundamental self-control. And this is what makes the American War for Independence different in nature from the revolutions and wars of alleged liberation which have followed it.

The Americans fought to *reclaim* their traditional rights as Englishmen. They did not resort to arms to fulfill the fantasies of some wild-eyed fanatic, but rather to preserve their own heritage and patrimony, which the political and commercial interests in Britain were intent on taking away. We can be sure that the colonists — the descendants and neighbors of those who risked their lives crossing the stormy Atlantic in fragile wooden vessels to secure, by their own efforts, a better life — knew well the value of liberty and property. In the Marxian climate in which we celebrate our bicentennial, I think this point can scarcely be overstressed.

We have had our derelictions, it is true. Individuals and groups have in the past opted for other "arrangements." But until recently in this nation's history, ideology never did prevail for long over common sense. We need only examine the documents of the time to see that even the estimable Pilgrim fathers had some alien ideas tucked away in their own baggage. You might even go so far as to say that communism came over on the Mayflower.

The full story of the First Thanksgiving in New England is an eloquent answer to those who pretend that mankind can be better served by more governmental controls, handouts, and restrictions. The Pilgrims actually tried the very thing that many politicians are advocating today. These Pilgrims nearly starved to death. Then they turned to God for an answer — and they got it.

It is not a well-known fact that the Pilgrims' experiment with communism failed within three years' time. In order to survive they had to turn to a system that rewarded individual initiative.

Before landing in Massachusetts, the Pilgrims entered into what is known as the Mayflower Compact. Under this covenant, Plymouth Colony was established as a share-the-wealth community. No one owned anything. Whatever was produced belonged to the community as a whole — to "all the people," as the modern politicians now put it.

The system was called, in the quaint writing of that day, "the comone course and condition." The Pilgrims lived under this system from the desperate, disease-ridden first winter of 1620–21 until the hungry spring of 1623. Then they changed to private enterprise.

Why? William Bradford, the second governor of Plymouth Colony, tells why in his book entitled *Of Plimoth Plantation*. Governor Bradford wrote that the Pilgrims weren't long under this so-called "comone course and condition" before it "was found to breed much confusion & discontent." Governor Bradford wrote that "work was retarded that would have been to [our] benefite and comforts." The Governor then explained that the young men who were most efficient and able to work had no incentive to produce, because they knew they would not be rewarded any more than the lazy or inefficient men in the colony.

So no one did any more work than he had to do. Instead of a Thanksgiving feast in the fall of 1622, there was literal starvation and hopelessly low morale. In his book Governor Bradford related what was done about this grim condition:

"So they begane to thinke how they might raise as much corne as they could . . . that they might not still thus languish in misere." The governor continued: "At last, after much debate of things, the governor [Bradford himself] gave way that they should set corne every man for his own perticular. . . . This had very good success, for it made all hands very industrious. . . . Much more corne was planted than other [wise] would have been."

The governor reflected on this incident. He condemned the theory that his people had tried and found wanting — the theory of socialism and communism: "As if —," Governor Bradford noted sadly, "As if they were wiser than God."

This is, I believe, the significance of Thanksgiving

that in the intervening centuries has become dim and obscure. But it is, to say the least, the story about the Pilgrims that should be taught in our schools. Today's headlines still publicize leaders among us who advocate that personal incentive and responsibility be abandoned by converting our traditional structure into a duplicate of systems that have been tried and have failed throughout history. Such systems will always fail because, as the Pilgrims learned at Plymouth Colony, they violate certain economic and moral laws that simply will not bend. As it has been said of the Ten Commandments, these are laws we cannot break; we can only break ourselves against them.

CHAPTER THREE

The State Religion

THE GREAT principle that the founders of our republic sought to establish in their political institutions is that progress consists in restraining the state. In devising the Constitution, they made every effort to see that political power was divided and circumscribed and that the rights of the individual were explicitly declared. The great aim of our republic, the concept that distinguished it from all the countries of the old world, was *preventing* the consolidation of political power.

This was in no way a crusade for "power to the people." The "people" whom politicians are forever extolling can be as tyrannical as any despot. The framers of the Constitution were meticulous to see that the rights of all Americans would be protected, and human freedom maximized, by rigorously limiting the authority of every branch of government and by taking every precaution to see that power blocs could not reconvene.

In doing so, the nation's founders revealed their profound respect for the law, which they saw not as a vehicle for social regeneration — for this is the work of God's grace — but as a restraint on the fallen nature of man.

It is a great irony and a perversion of language that in our times the persons who would use the law for a com-

25

pletely different purpose are commonly known as "liberals." There was a time, a century ago, when a liberal by definition was one who opted for a political program that did indeed seek less government rather than more.

This is not true today.

While still under the camouflage of a name that implies freedom, modern "liberals" are always seeking to undo the work of centuries. Without exception their creed and their platforms call for the enactment of ever more laws.

In the last thirty years or so, the doctrines of the liberals — and particularly their concept of the law — have become ever more imbedded in the thinking of our opinion makers and legislators. Since coming to the Senate, I have been able to see, every day, these demolition crews at work, dynamiting the foundations of our liberties on the pretext of accomplishing some overriding social good.

I do not propose to state here in detail how this philosophy came to have such dominance in our country, but only to point out the incompatibility of liberalism with political freedom and biblical morality. Liberalism is the political creed of a pseudo-religion known as humanism, which grew out of the Renaissance in Europe. Humanism, which is basically an attempt to create a heaven on earth — a heaven with God and His law excluded from it — drew freely from the ancient pagan religions and philosophies that Christianity had supplanted many centuries before.

The television commercial that urges the viewers to buy a certain alcoholic beverage on the rationale that since they pass this way but once, they should grab all the pleasure they can, is an expression of humanist values. The pagans expressed it with a little more elegance: "Eat, drink, and be merry, for tomorrow we die." This preoccupation with the pleasures and the pains of this life is absolutely incompatible with the Christian view of life.

A great deal of violence has been done to the Constitution, in ways I will later endeavor to describe, by individuals whose alleged objective has been to preserve the separation of church and state. The most conspicuous of their accomplishments is the court-ordered suppression of voluntary prayer in the public schools. This development many liberals applaud, and it is typical of the way they deal with other people's freedom.

Yet if liberals were consistent in their position, their objections to Bible reading and the Lord's Prayer would apply also to the doctrines of secular humanism that have become, in everything but name, the state religion. Traditional Christian beliefs and practices are being replaced by a religion sewn together from scraps of Karl Marx, Sigmund Freud, John Maynard Keynes, John Dewey, and other socialist gurus whose thinking is so congenial to the liberal mind and so flattering to the conceit of our natures.

The new religion is, to sum it up, collectivist, totalitarian, and implacably hostile to the family, the church, and free institutions. It claims dedicated adherents in politics, in communications and education, in business and industry. In short, the new religion makes a god of government.

Indeed so rooted are the presumptions of this counterfeit religion, and so universal is the idea that Congress has only to pass enough laws and appropriate enough money to achieve any purpose under the heavens, that millions of people scarcely bother to question the ethical and moral foundations of their political beliefs.

But those who do are sometimes startled to find that liberalism — rather than being a vehicle for advancing human welfare — is actually the greatest possible obstacle to that end. The reason is that liberals see their fellowmen in primarily economic terms, continually classifying those who are poor or affluent or disadvantaged or underprivileged or whatever. This categorizing of human beings primarily according to their material means is a distortion of their dignity and reduces this philosophy to a narrow economic doctrine. The liberal believes in setting certain economic and social goals and then so arranging the organization of the government as to compel its citizens to achieve these goals.

The true conservative, on the other hand, acknowledges the economic and material side of man's nature, but always gives primacy to the spiritual and moral dimension. Man is a creature comprised of body and soul, and this truth is the basis for the uniqueness of every person.

Throughout history, conservatives have taken a dim view of state-sponsored schemes that seek to regiment human beings like so many ants in a colony. It is the separateness of individuals and their utterly distinctive gifts and potential that must be respected in the arrangements of civil society.

Conservatives believe that government begins with the individual and proceeds to the family. The ultimate government is the dominion of God. In between we find the state, whose purpose is to regulate specific dealings among nations and men. What has grown up in the last two generations is the utterly erroneous belief that the civil government should take precedence over the family, the church, and every other form of social organization, based on some misguided concepts about "equality" or "democracy" or "racial balance."

It is an indication of how far we have gone on the path to totalitarianism that today the term *government* almost always refers to the federal colossus. And while I do not mean to belabor this difference in outlook, it is these conflicting views of the nature of man and the nature of law that underlie the dilemma of modern politics.

The true conservative believes that the Declaration of Independence and the Constitution are unique and glorious documents because they establish, in a way unprecedented in human history, the best conditions for fulfilling the scriptural admonition to render unto Caesar the things that are Caesar's and to God the things that are God's.

CHAPTER FOUR

Freedom Is the Basis of Prosperity

IF GEORGE Washington is the father of our country, the father of our economic system is Adam Smith.

In his great book, *The Wealth of Nations* — written, coincidentally, in 1776 — Smith described a system in which individuals would be free to use their skills and talents and their property — their capital, we would say — to produce goods for the market. The buyers likewise would have the widest opportunity to exercise their own judgment as to what items at what price were worth the expenditure of their money.

Thus the most efficient and adventurous entrepreneurs would be rewarded with the greatest patronage and profit. By a process of selection, the inefficient and inferior would be weeded out. The producer and the consumer, without the intrusion of extraneous controls, would work toward the mutual advantage of both. It was a system based on freedom, not coercion, and the extraordinarily high standard of living that Americans have enjoyed for generations is a direct outgrowth of the concept of the free marketplace.

Just when a person would think the point had been made triumphantly for all time that *freedom is the only basis for prosperity*, a strange thing happened. American intellectuals, influenced by the Fabian Socialists in

England, grew more and more interested in the political manipulation of the economy. Thus, using the "general welfare" clause of the Constitution as a wedge, the New Dealers were able to initiate the first wedge of government controls over agriculture. The camel's nose was in the tent, and the fatal precedent of government intervention in the marketplace was set for life.

It has always dismayed — if not surprised — me to note that the most insidious assaults on our economy have occurred, not in the marketplace, but in the classrooms of colleges and universities. Today we have a generation prepared in effect to repudiate its heritage.

It is rare indeed to find an academic who has anything good to say about free enterprise generally, or the profit motive specifically. What an irony this is, when you consider that the hundreds of colleges and universities in the United States are directly or indirectly maintained by the proceeds of our system.

For many intellectuals, some form of socialism is vastly preferable to the workings of the unpredictable free market, which responds every day to the decisions of millions of persons acting individually.

I recall an incident that took place not too long ago in my own state of North Carolina. I hesitate to single out a particular university, but the incident is doubtless typical of many across the land.

A young man of my acquaintance, a student at North Carolina State University, signed up for a history course. But after purchasing the first textbook assigned to his class, he dropped the course and selected another in its place. Life is too short, he told a friend, to spend one's time listening to someone's opinion that the principles of the United States' economic system are wrong and should be overthrown.

I felt that the young man should have remained in the class. I thought his voice was needed to argue in favor of the capitalistic, free enterprise system in America. One thing is for certain: Somebody needs to do it.

The first two words of the textbook's introduction are "Capitalism stinks." From there the authors move into 458 pages of absolute denunciation of America. The title of the book is *Up Against the American Myth*. The text begins by declaring, "We can only solve our social problems . . . by doing away with capitalism and the institutions that support it." This, the authors maintain, "is the point of this book, and we make it again and again."

Indeed they do. It is difficult to believe that such a violent diatribe against America would be assigned as a mandatory textbook for students at a state university.

What does the textbook advocate to replace the American free enterprise, capitalistic system which, students are supposed to believe, must be done away with? Turn to most any page for an answer. At random I opened to page 439: " . . . it is only through developing and expanding [the] socialist rationality that the advanced industrial countries can hope to overcome [the ills of society]."

Throughout this textbook there is an unrelenting drumfire of denunciation of America. The United States is repeatedly described as "imperialistic." Our system, we discover, is deliberately operated to oppress the people. Only socialism can correct the thousand and one ills that plague the country, if one is to believe this textbook. Sadly all too many young people do.

I telephoned the young instructor who taught the course and who assigned the textbook. He is a graduate of Yale. What, I asked him, would he recommend to replace capitalism in America? Socialism, perhaps? He hedged. "*None* of the systems works," he finally replied. Then he qualified his response: "Oh, capitalism works for some people, but it doesn't work for others."

He bristled momentarily at the suggestion that it was capitalism that had built the university at which he teaches and that it was capitalism that provides his salary. "I cannot," he said, "accept that theory."

The conversation, though polite, was pointless.

Here was a young man, an instructor at a great university built and maintained by the people, who made clear that he agreed in substance with the first two words of the textbook he had assigned to his students. "Capitalism stinks." And only socialism can supply a solution to the problems of mankind.

In parting, I inquired whether there was a textbook he planned to assign which suggests that capitalism does not stink, and I suggested one written by a famous economist. He was candid! No, the name of Ludwig von Mises was not familiar to him, yet von Mises was the country's leading scholar in free market economics.

So history students at N.C. State University were assigned a textbook declaring that the economic system upon which their country was built is a system that "stinks." And interestingly, this textbook was written by three militantly radical graduate students at Harvard — Tom Christoffel, David Finkelhor, and Dan Gilbarg. One can only wonder "what meat these radicals eat" in the Ivy League that makes them so venomously condemn and revile America.

Few students go to college prepared to do battle with such confirmed leftists at the lectern. I received a letter from a sophomore who claimed that one of his professors, in an informal discussion, commented that the free enterprise system is falling apart because of — in the professor's words — "the inequities it breeds."

"I wish," my young friend wrote me, "that you would provide an answer for this observation, for frankly it worries me that most successful rock musicians, for example, are paid more money in one night than a college professor earns in a year."

This is my answer. In the first place, the indictment is misdirected. If, under the free enterprise system, an entertainer prospers more than a teacher, a publisher of comic books more than those who produce poetry, or manufacturers of cosmetics more than painters of fine art — it is not the economic system that needs changing.

The changes must be made in the allegiances and sense of values of men. To condemn free enterprise is merely to make it a scapegoat for failures on a much deeper level. The obvious response to the college student's question is that improving society's sense of values is not a matter of controlling the economy, but of deepening the sense of individual responsibility.

Then, those who would discard the free enterprise system or refashion it in the shape of a partially or totally socialistic state are simply ignorant of history.

There have been, and there still are, abuses and injustices. But even so, the free men of this free capitalistic economy outcreated and outproduced, in six generations covering a short span of 200 years, all of the combined efforts of men in the preceding 6,000 years. It seems obvious, therefore, that we need to stop apologizing for free enterprise. Notwithstanding its shortcomings, it is curious logic to assume that the way to correct these faults lies in destroying the system and substituting for it a government-controlled economy.

Men do not become saints merely by being put in charge of a government bureau. Further, in our own generation we have seen that governmental intrusion upon private affairs has resulted in a drastic curtailment of individual responsibility and initiative. The contrast between the productive capacity of the United States and Soviet Russia is a dramatic example of this. Even today, "detente" is, from the U.S. point of view, nothing but a welfare program for the Soviets.

Consider this, that socialism is not a means of creating and distributing wealth; it is merely a way of creating and enforcing poverty. One can draw no other conclusion when he weighs the ultimate effect of the Marxist principle, "From each according to his ability; to each according to his need."

The professor's remark that the free enterprise system is falling apart is probably another case in which the wish was father to the thought. Some would tear the system apart in the belief that responsible freedom can be improved upon. But those who hold such beliefs should ponder the alternative to free enterprise: indeed, they should behold the effects of the inroads already made into it. Any system such as socialism or communism, or diluted or disguised variations of them, does nothing but reduce the incentive of men by taking away from them the fruits of their labors. And this in turn destroys the creativity and productivity of men.

Some years ago a clergyman found himself addressing a gathering in Charlotte, North Carolina, and the talk turned to economics. "As far as socialism is concerned," he said, "there are only two places where it will work: in heaven, where they don't need it, and in hell, where they have it already." How apt. How succinct.

For all its faults, the free enterprise system has produced a higher standard of living, more innovations and conveniences and miracles of technology, more culture, more leisure, and a higher degree of religious freedom than is found anywhere else in the world today. We should stop and ponder the fact that in this country we define poverty at an income level higher than the median income in that worker's paradise, the Soviet Union.

Certainly there are inequities, but free men are more likely to correct them than bureaucrats or slaves. Certainly our sense of values in this country is sometimes subject to criticism. But who stands a better chance of correcting it than free men?

Free enterprise is a tool that can be used properly or abused. The professor who criticized it was not really talking about the system, but about himself and the rest of us. The free enterprise system does not deserve to be discarded or even refashioned. It needs a recognition of what it is, what it has done, and what it can do.

CHAPTER FIVE

The Profit Motive

ACADEMICS ARE by no means the only persons who look upon the profit motive as crude and uncouth. Many others who consider themselves high-minded people, if not specifically intellectuals, consider the profit motive something dispensable or obsolete or archaic. They think we have outgrown it.

I once asked a gentleman who felt this way what would be the alternative to the profit motive. His rejoinder was full of benevolence, of altruism, of wishes of good things for everybody.

The man suggested that modern scientific and technological discoveries eventually will provide a life of ease and comfort for all. The trouble with this theory — assuming for the sake of argument that it is true — is that it doesn't suggest who will do the work and meet the cost in the meantime.

Parenthetically I might add that this sentimental and simple belief in a brave new world is one of the oldest delusions that has descended on man. Medieval writers frequently told of a fabulous Land of Cockaigne, full of the medieval equivalent of pie-in-the-sky, where nobody had to work for a living.

Neither the medievals, nor the moderns — with their unshakable faith in technology, leisure, and abundance for everybody — answer the question of who will provide the incentive for the discoveries that will convert the world into a paradise. Who will plant the potatoes?

If it seems tedious to dwell on such practical matters, then I am making my point. Not everyone has a firm grasp of the obvious fact that the profit motive has been responsible for much of the progress our nation has made. This is the difference between America's mass production and comforts and conveniences, and the primitive tribal conditions in the Australian Outback. It is the difference between our own well-stocked supermarkets and the endless lining up and waiting by housewives to purchase a slice of ham or a loaf of bread in the state-run shops of Eastern Europe.

A Polish refugee now living in this country wrote a memoir of his first days in Chicago. He was incredulous that he could walk into any market he chose and buy all the ham he wanted. In Poland, ham was tightly rationed and exported by the government, so the Polish people, who produce excellent ham, hardly ever tasted it.

In this country, men have learned that if they work a little harder, think a little clearer, and produce a little more efficiently, they will be able to earn more, save more, and acquire more of the comforts and pleasures of life, whether they are employees or employers.

There is nothing materialistic about this attitude. It is entirely in keeping with the biblical parable of the talents. The profit motive becomes materialistic only when a man ignores his other responsibilities to himself, his Creator, and his fellowman. The basic motivation for the free market is individual initiative, and paradoxically this brings with it inestimable benefits to society at large. If you are looking for a system based on envy and greed — something with all the grossest aspects of materialism — then you want socialism.

Moreover, to contend that the profit motive is old-fashioned and archaic is refuted by the example of the intellectual community itself. Why would an individual seek advanced degrees if not to enhance his own knowledge and worth? Yet it is true today, as it was in biblical times, that a learned man with no incentive is as much without hope as the man with no talents.

Let there be no doubt: the alternative to the profit motive is the socialist state. History shows that no nation has survived for very long when its citizens were denied the profit motive. The police power of these states has had to be immeasurably enhanced to compel their citizens to work.

The truth is that today's young people are accustomed to modern comforts. Most of them, unless they have the misfortune to fall into the negativism of the avant-garde, not only want to continue to enjoy them; they also want to improve and increase them. In their doing so, our society will move closer to that life of ease and comfort that my old acquaintance envisions.

But this will happen because of the profit motive he considers beneath his dignity, not in spite of it. And the process will be retarded only to the extent that government imposes the restraints of confiscatory taxation and controls that impede progress — oddly enough, in the name of progress — and kill the incentive of men to strive for a better way of life.

CHAPTER SIX

And What of the Role of Business?

SOME TIME AGO, a prominent citizen of my hometown appeared before a local civic club with a stirring and eloquent defense of America's free enterprise system. We must stop, he insisted, this trend of introducing ever more federal control into every imaginable aspect of our lives and businesses. It was certainly an impressive declaration, and the gentleman was rewarded with a loud ovation.

One hour and fifteen minutes later, the same gentleman appeared before his city council, heading a delegation of equally prominent citizens who had come to urge their city government to make application to Washington for federal funds. They had in mind a project that they considered most worthy. All the same, it was a project designed to put the city government and the federal government in competition with private enterprise.

Just as the temperance leader who is a secret alcoholic does far more damage to his cause than the chronic inebriate, the businessman who calls for concessions, monopolies, controls, and regulations that especially favor his industry is doing mortal damage to the concept of free enterprise. Free enterprise has to be free — continually and honestly and completely. No product and no man's labor ought to be artificially propped up or protected in price. If the system is permitted to function, it will serve the interests of all of society better than any short-term reliance on government devices and controls.

Economist Milton Friedman once remarked that the great enemies of free enterprise are businessmen and intellectuals — businessmen, because they want socialism for themselves and free enterprise for everyone else; intellectuals, because they want free enterprise for themselves and socialism for everyone else.

Considered in the abstract, federal regulation and control are universally denounced. Our whole economy is papered over with edicts and quotas and a superfluity of laws. And while everyone will agree that most of them are wasteful and unnecessary, there is hardly a businessman or a trade representative or a union official who will not leap like a trout to protect the special legislation that spares him "unfair competition" or "lowered standards" or what have you.

All of us in government, in business, and in private life must come, one of these days, to an understanding of what this overregulation is costing our economy. At this moment, a tremendous federal bureaucracy presides over what remains of our free enterprise system. Great corporations and small businesses both find it necessary to support bureaucracies of their own to see that their operations conform to a flood of edicts and guidelines.

In these instances, individuals are taken out of the productive economy for the purpose of filling out forms. The shareholders and taxpayers are put to the expense of office buildings, salaries, telephones, coffee breaks, and paper clips.

I well remember the furor that arose when Charles Wilson, the former president of General Motors and Secretary of Defense in the Eisenhower Administration, reportedly made the remark, "What is good for General Motors is good for the country." Not since the days of Marie Antoinette has a supposed offhand remark generated as much obloquy and denunciation. What Mr. Wilson actually said, however, was "What's good for America is good for General Motors." That is a statement of pure truth which needs no defense from me.

One does not have to observe the Congress very long to find there a profoundly anti-business bias. Not only have the environmentalists and the consumerists declared open season on American business, but the politicians are rushing in to win votes by denouncing American businessmen and industrialists as devils of the deepest dye.

The attack on business is nothing other than an attack on the basic principles of free enterprise. Almost a generation of neo-Marxist teaching in the public schools has convinced millions of Americans that there is something wrong about being a success in the marketplace.

This nation's people need to be reminded that the greatest antipoverty agency of all time is a business that turns a profit. And businessmen have got to take the lead in practicing and defending the economic principles that have made our country prosperous and free.

Many companies are conducting excellent public relations programs to teach basic free market economics to the public. This is a highly praiseworthy undertaking, notwithstanding the hostile and cynical reaction these efforts sometimes arouse in the leftist media.

A pioneer in this effort is a company in Los Angeles, the Coast Savings & Loan Association, which at one time operated a "Free Enterprise Department." This was well staffed full-time by several employees who produced and distributed hundreds of thousands of pieces of literature every month explaining the advantages of the free enterprise system in America.

The Association published a booklet entitled "The Ideological War: Communist Myths and American Truths." In clear, concise language, this booklet cites hundreds of popular political cliches and then answers them. Here are some examples:

And What of the Role of Business?

Myth: The more complex the society, the more government control we need.

Truth: The more complex the society, the more we should rely on the self-adapting process of men acting freely. No single mind or group of minds is capable of understanding the many activities of a simple society, much less a complex one.

Myth: Capitalism has failed; now the government must step in and save us.

Truth: The only spheres where capitalism is failing are where the government has already stepped in.

Myth: The government should provide security for all.

Truth: The promise of cradle-to-grave security has weakened our economic incentive, tending to make men financially irresponsible and reducing them to low levels of morality. Look around the country at what is happening, if you doubt this.

Myth: We need to increase the rate of our productive growth through government participation, controls, and regulation.

Truth: The United States is living proof of a country starting underdeveloped and becoming, through free enterprise, the greatest nation in the world. Why should we give up an economic system that works for one which fails? We do not live to grow; we grow to live better.

Myth: Increasing consumption causes increased prosperity.

Truth: Prosperity results from higher productivity per man-hour.

Myth: Inflation is necessary to prevent depressions.

Truth: Inflation causes depressions. Inflation is like a drug: it brings temporary good feelings followed by a depression. Overdoses of either drugs or inflation cause death.

Myth: Corporations earn from 40 to 50 cents profit on each sales dollar.

Truth: Corporations make an average of three cents profit out of each sales dollar.

Myth: The government can operate a business cheaper, because it makes no profit.

Truth: In competition with private enterprise, the businesses being operated by the government are so inefficient that they are losing many billions of dollars a year.

And the final example:

Myth: Only the rich can save money.

Truth: Only those who save can become rich.

And that, as they say in the vernacular, is telling it like it is.

CHAPTER SEVEN

Taxation!

AN AXIOM of politics quoted far less often than it ought to be is that the power to tax involves the power to destroy. We underrate the importance of the fact that it was the issue of taxation — nominal taxes on stamps and tea — that ignited the fuse that detonated the War for Independence. As more than one commentator has pointed out, if the colonists thought that taxation without representation was so bad, they ought to see what you get *with* representation.

Some time ago a researcher added up the number of taxes levied on a pair of shoes from the time the leather left the cow until the shoes were sold at a retail shop. When every possible direct and indirect tax was taken into account, the total amounted to well over two hundred different tax levies. On a far more complex project — such as a new house — the taxes, direct and indirect, are so numerous that about one-third of the price of a new house can be attributed to taxes or to government regulations in one guise or another.

Charles Dickens's *Tale of Two Cities* leaves vivid impressions of the turmoil in Paris that led to the French Revolution. There, too, though there was plenty of combustible material lying about to feed that conflagration, it was the issue of taxation that sent the French government and nation up in flames.

About half a century before the birth of Christ, the great orator, Marcus Tullius Cicero, had some remarks to make before the Roman Senate. Ponder his words and measure them for yourself against the predicament of the United States in 1976.

"We are taxed," Cicero complained, "in our bread and in our wine, in our incomes and our investments, on our land and on our property, not only for base creatures who do not deserve the name of man, but for foreign nations, for complacent nations who will bow to us and accept our largesse and promise to assist us in the keeping of the peace — these mendicant nations who will destroy us when we show a moment of weakness or when our treasury is bare, and surely it is becoming bare. We are taxed to maintain legions on their soil. . . . We keep them in precarious balance only with our gold. . . . They take our very flesh and they hate and despise us."

But the senators rejected Cicero's warning. Rome continued to follow the advice more recently immortalized by the late Harry Hopkins — tax and tax, spend and spend, elect and elect.

As the liberties of the Romans were compromised one after another in the name of emergencies, Cicero stood again before the Senate for his second oration:

"I tell you that freedom does not mean the freedom to exploit the law in order to destroy it. It is not freedom which permits the Trojan horse to be wheeled within the gates. He who espouses tyranny and oppression is against [his country]. He who plots against established authority and incites the people to violence is against [his country]."

The Roman law code, like our own Constitution, contained a reference to the "general welfare" of the people. Cicero warned the senators not to misinterpret the word *welfare*. Under that phrase, he told them, "all sorts of excesses can be employed by lusting tyrants to make us all slaves." The politicians of Rome listened politely, ignored his advice, and then proceeded to use the treasury to buy the political support of the masses. The doom of Rome was sealed.

But Cicero continued to plead for the restoration of integrity and sanity to his government. Finally, at a time when troubles were coming thick and fast upon Rome, Cicero was banished. At the end of his trial, he said:

"You have succeeded against me. Be it as you will. I will depart. For this day's work, Lords, you have encouraged treason and opened the prison doors to free the traitors. A nation can survive its fools . . . but the traitor moves among those within the gates freely, his sly whispers rustling through the alleys, heard in the very halls of government itself. He rots the very soul of a nation; he works secretly and unknown in the night to undermine the [fundamentals of a nation]; he infects the body politic so that it can no longer resist."

More than one observer of the political scene has pointed out that nothing comes easier than spending the public money. It appears to belong to nobody, and the temptation is overwhelming to confer it on somebody. In the past forty years, surely no power has been so much abused by the Congress as the power of the purse. The U. S. Treasury was instituted to receive tax money to pay the nation's legitimate bills, but it has become El Dorado for swarms of ambitious politicians. One politician told me — and there is no doubt he believed it — that money will make iron float.

Consequently the taxation of our people has become so burdensome that today the average taxpayer must hand over to federal, state, and local governments a growing percentage of his earned income. According to the Tax Foundation, the typical taxpayer works from January 1 to April 30 solely for the benefit of the government. Only after May 1 does he start earning money for himself. Taxes are the largest item in the family budget, and more than food and housing combined.

It is sometimes hard to realize that within the lifetime of many of us there was no personal income tax in this country. What is more, when the Constitution was amended to permit the federal government to impose the income tax, it was clear that the Congress did not dream it would ever reach the proportions that we face today.

In fact, the senators who fought hardest on behalf of the tax were confident that the government would never take more than two or three percent of a person's taxable income. Throughout the record of the debates in the Congress, such assurances are found repeatedly. To read them today is bitter irony indeed.

A prominent lawyer of that time traveled the country, pleading in vain against the constitutional amendment. He told audiences that if the government could levy a tax of 2 percent, it might one day levy a tax of 25, 50, or even 90 or 100 percent.

The late Senator Borah arose in the Senate one day to ridicule this lawyer, Joseph Choate.

"Who," asked Senator Borah, "would levy such a tax? Whose equity, sense of fairness, of justice, of patriotism, does Mr. Choate question?"

And then Senator Borah answered his own question: "Why, [he is questioning the integrity of] the representatives of the American people!"

Senator Borah's colleagues laughed at the very idea.

"Not only that," said Senator Borah, but Mr. Choate is questioning "the intelligence, the fairness, the justice of the people themselves, to whom their representatives are always answerable."

Senator Borah was a famous and able man, but in this case he could hardly have been more wrong — as most Americans rediscover every April 15. The Congress approved the income tax idea, in the form of the Sixteenth Amendment, on July 12, 1909. The amendment received the necessary ratification by the states on February 3, 1913. On that dark day, the people of this country began to lose their freedom. From then on, the Congress has known where and how to get the money to push its citizens around. An income tax of 50 percent now applies at levels far removed from great wealth. And in the top bracket the tax is 70 percent — only 30 percent short of the total expropriation that Joseph Choate, the apprehensive lawyer, feared.

The amount of your taxes, as everyone should realize by now, is something over which you have very little control. You can exert it only by controlling government, instead of permitting it to control you. There is the inevitable relationship between what the government spends and what it takes from you. The relationship cannot be avoided except by the dangerous and immoral practice of deficit spending — that is, by permitting the government to spend more than it takes in. This is nothing but borrowing against the futures of our children and grandchildren. There is no such thing as something for nothing.

I have heard recently from several obviously distressed citizens who acknowledged that they had had their first real confrontation with what they regarded as confiscatory taxation. Each person in his own way described himself as a citizen of modest means who had worked and saved and now possessed only one investment of any real substance, a piece of land. Each of them had proposed to sell his land and use the money for living expenses during the coming years of retirement.

None of these citizens had reckoned with the sweeping hand of the tax collector. All their letters expressed astonishment at how much of the sale price of their land they would be forced to turn over to the government. One of them concluded his letter with the remark, "It's slavery, that's what it is!"

Society may not unanimously agree that this is slavery. But the burden of taxation is a fact of economic life that all too many will ignore, in this day of ever-increasing governmental spending, until it is too late to rectify the situation without social upheaval. The attitude of the people has been carefully fashioned, step by step, to accept first this additional tax and then that one, until, as the gentlemen wrote, there is a sort of national unconsciousness about how great a tax burden the people are really bearing.

All sorts of devices have been contrived: withholding taxes, Social Security taxes, excise taxes ad infinitum, all designed to get the most possible feathers from the goose with the fewest possible squawks. All the while there have been deceptive soothing syrups in the form of political promises and great doses of bureaucratic boasts about what the government is doing for the people.

This is precisely the way slaveholders in centuries gone by kept peace among their slaves. It was all perfectly legal, this business of some men controlling the lives of many other men, of requiring men to work to provide money for others to spend as they wished. It was a splendid practice of freedom — for everybody except the slaves. So also the deceptive business of "withholding taxes" blinds many men to the reality of their servitude to the tax collector.

Back in the sixties an interesting experiment in psychology was conducted, if memory serves, by an employer in Missouri. For several months he paid his employees in cash. He deducted nothing for taxes. Instead he required each employee to step immediately to the next window and pay the taxes that normally would have been withheld.

By the time the second payday rolled around, he noticed a remarkable increase in his employees' interest in governmental affairs, especially government spending. By the end of the second month, he said, his employees were writing to their congressmen and senators demanding that government spending be cut.

This was a dramatic lesson in practical civics. The same point was made in a different way by another employer. Instead of making regular weekly deductions, this man paid all his employees their full wages for the first three weeks of each month. The employees were delighted at this unexpected windfall. But at the end of the fourth week, the employer deducted taxes for all four weeks. This meant, of course, that most of the employees received at most only a few dollars for their week's work. Some did not come out even that well: they *owed the company!* These employees likewise developed a healthy interest in governmental affairs.

I have no idea what the IRS said about these experiments. Indeed a bureaucrat who saw his job endangered would probably declare the experiments illegal.

I have no wish to demean the idea that all citizens should welcome the responsibility to share in the support of the *proper* functions of government, properly conducted. Yet the crazy-quilt assortment of governmental programs and iniquitous exceptions and exemptions that lie outside the framework of limited government which Jefferson and his fellow patriots ordained constitute an immense drain on the productive capacity of this country.

How many of today's so-called federal aid programs do you suppose the founding fathers would have approved, even in the context of today's conditions? Would they not have counseled — in fact, did not they explicitly warn us — that the money for such things had to come from somewhere? And anyone who doubts where the money comes from has only to visit his local post office on the fifteenth of April.

CHAPTER EIGHT

Budget

PART OF the folklore of the Congress is that each year the proposed federal budget is delivered to the office of each senator and congressman. The reasoning behind this custom, which dates back for generations, is that members of Congress were supposed to know what they were voting on, the federal budget included.

Now the federal budget for each fiscal year consumes thousands of printed pages — big pages, mind you, with small type — listing the amounts of money that the federal government is spending.

The way I figure it, hardly a member of Congress for the last thirty years has had the vaguest notion about the contents of this budget. Put yourself in a congressman's shoes. Suppose you were assigned to study hundreds of pages of budget figures, and suppose you were to devote one hour of study to each million dollars of proposed expenditure. That seems like a reasonable amount of time to devote to the proposal to spend a million dollars, doesn't it?

Well, if you started when the budget was submitted, and you worked twenty-four hours a day, seven days a week, fifty-two weeks a year, you would not be ready to vote on the FY 1977 budget until July 21, 2020. It would take you that long to study the budget at a million dollars an hour.

The point is that we have long since lost hope of any

supervision by our elected representatives in the Congress of the amounts of money being spent by the federal government. When we talk of the "democratic process," we are talking nonsense where government spending is involved.

More than a century ago, a noted French economist and statesman, Alexis de Tocqueville, visited the United States. Our nation had not even celebrated its centennial at that time, but it was already becoming, economically and politically, the marvel of the world. De Tocqueville studied carefully the new concept that he found here. He went home to write admiringly of the unique system that had so captivated his attention. But he stated a prophecy: It wouldn't last.

It would fail, de Tocqueville said, because sooner or later the American people would embrace a political system that would encourage politicians to promise something for nothing, and that would mark the downfall of America.

He wrote that the "supreme power" of government would eventually "cover the surface of society with a network of rules and regulations that would stupefy the people until the nation is reduced to nothing better than a flock of timid and industrious animals of whom the government is the shepherd."

But de Tocqueville did not foresee two developments: this same flock of American taxpayers would be fleeced by the patrons of the indolent and unproductive of this country; and the federal government, like the *conquistadores* of old, would exploit the American worker so as to subsidize almost every other country in the world.

For a century and a half, our country for the most part adhered to the ideals of limited and frugal government that were reemphasized in the farewell address of President George Washington.

As he left office on September 19, 1796, Washington exhorted his countrymen:

"Avoid likewise the accumulation of debt, not only

by shunning occasions of expense, but by vigorous exertion in time of peace to discharge the debts which unavoidable wars may have occasioned, not ungenerously throwing upon posterity the burden which we ourselves ought to bear."

In living up to these ideals, we built up a great industrial economy and enjoyed the benefits of a sound and stable dollar.

In the first 111 years of our national existence, the federal government of the United States spent $16.5 billion; in the next 40 years (1901-1940), the government spent $149.5 billion. From 1941 to 1950, the federal government spent $535 billion. From 1951 to 1960, it spent $744 billion. From 1961 to 1970, it spent $1.4 trillion. And from 1971 to 1977, the federal government will have spent $2.1 trillion.

Naturally these figures are beyond comprehension, even to the senators and congressmen who vote for them so easily. But the difference between a million and a billion is easier to visualize if you think of it in terms of everyday life. If a man sent his wife out on a shopping spree to spend a million dollars at the rate of one thousand dollars a day, she would return in a little over three years. But if he sent his wife out with a billion dollars to spend, she wouldn't come back for three thousand years.

Thus the first $100 billion budget was not drawn up until 1945, and then it was under the stimulus of a world war. It took 156 years to reach that level of spending. The first $200 billion budget was not formed until 1971; it took only 26 years to reach that level. The first $300 billion budget was reached in 1975; this time it took only four years. And as this is written, a $400 billion budget is projected for fiscal 1977; it took only two years this time.

But the level of spending by itself is not enough for comment. The fact is that the spending increases were fueled by increasing deficits, as high as $76 billion in 1976 alone. That deficit — for just one year — is as much as the whole government spent per year when I first came to

Washington as a Senate aide in the 1950s. The projected total federal debt for the fiscal year ahead, 1977, stands at $719.5 billion, almost twice the proposed federal budget.

In the fiscal avalanche let loose in the last decade, we have arrived at the point where the largest expenditure in the federal budget is not spent by the Defense Department, nor is it spent by the Treasury to pay the salaries of U.S. employees. The greatest part of the budget consists of what economists label "transfer payments" — or to put it bluntly, the money the government takes from one citizen to subsidize another.

Gradually, right before our eyes, the government has changed from an institution pledged to defend and enforce our liberties to a dispenser of "benefits." Such government "benefits," covering everything from Social Security to unemployment insurance, welfare programs, school lunches, and Medicare, add up to $177.1 billion, or 44 percent of the current budget. One out of every seven Americans is thus a beneficiary of federal income-redistribution schemes.

We need not belabor these figures to appreciate the shift of seismic proportions in the nature and function of government. And the authors of this immensely enhanced role of government — or what we might well call socialism-by-the-back-door — have been the liberal majority in the U.S. Congress.

As an example of how this was done, let us consider the food stamp program. During the days of the War on Poverty, numerous open-ended programs were enacted which, though they looked like tiny mustard seeds at the outset, have become immense trees in the fiscal forest.

Ostensibly as a program to combat malnutrition, the government began distributing food stamps in 1966 at an annual cost of $34 million. At this writing the food stamp program has become a colossal boondoggle, in which just about one in four Americans can qualify to have his grocery bills subsidized by the federal treasury. Its budget now runs at the rate of $6 billion, or roughly half the annual budget of the Department of Agriculture. What this immense sum is doing to inflate the price of food in the marketplace is very clear to anyone who goes to the grocery store.

Obviously the unproductive in our society cannot indefinitely increase their demands on the productive. Roy L. Ash, former Director of the Office of Management and Budget, projected what these trends portend for our economy in the next quarter-century:

"If transfer payments continue to increase at the rate they have . . . and if the GNP continues to rise at 3.5 percent a year (although some say this is an optimistic assumption) and if defense and all other federal spending is held to only a 1 percent annual growth for 25 years, then the federal budget for the year 2000 would be $1.4 trillion, in current dollars, four times the present level and nearly 40 percent of the then annual GNP. Furthermore, transfer payments, the redistribution-of-income function, will in that not-so-distant year comprise 80 percent of all federal dollars spent, compared to 20 percent in 1950 and over 50 percent today."

Mr. Ash concluded that unless we intervene to change things, in just a few more decades government at all levels will command over half this country's GNP. Some will argue that the economy is not harmed by the growth in transfer payments to almost any level: the money is spent, and goods and services are produced and purchased.

But, stressed Mr. Ash, this is also true of socialist countries, where goods and services are produced and employment is maintained. The critical difference is one of *freedom*.

"Should the worker-producer have and control most of the income realized by his labor, or should he hand it over to the control of government to, in turn, redistribute it to others to spend?" Mr. Ash asks.

"For, at some point, a bending reed will break. How

much of a worker's income need be taken from him before he loses his motivation to work? Or before he decides he'd be better off as the non-working recipient of a transfer payment himself? When that point is reached, who will do the production?"

We do not need to speculate about the distant future to realize we are on a path to a dead end. We are creating in this country the same conditions that have reduced postwar Britain to penury and stagnation.

A swelling chorus of demands for "benefits" of every conceivable sort coupled with the ruinous taxation and expropriation of whole segments of the economy has bent Britain double. A once great nation has been reduced to near bankruptcy and a negligible influence in world affairs.

Fifty years of socialism have impoverished the country, dispersed its empire, squandered its capital, and crushed its once magnificent spirit. And as diminishing returns continue to roll in, there is a new truculence and militance in the all-powerful labor unions. Britain today is a far cry from the worker's paradise the Fabian Socialists envisioned when they set up the machinery for this brave new world.

It is a matter of open discussion in the papers that communism is on the rise in Britain — the last step on the road to the Welfare State.

All Americans need to ponder well the implications of a supertaxing, superspending supergovernment. The Secretary of the Treasury summed up the situation recently when he said that we have more government than we want, more government than we need, and certainly more government than anyone is willing to pay for. All Americans who have swallowed the bait of government "benefits" need to be reminded that a government that is strong enough to give us everything we need is strong enough to take away everything we've got.

CHAPTER NINE

Inflation

FOR THE time being, let us accept the description President Ford gave to inflation when he called it Public Enemy Number One. (For myself, I think that distinction has been well earned by the entrenched inflation lobby in the Congress.)

Almost everyone perceives the dangers of inflation and feels the effects at every turn. The rocketing cost of everything we buy, the diminished value of savings and pensions, the anxiety and frayed tempers as paychecks no longer cover the necessities of life — these are everywhere experienced. The universality of this phenomenon and the many ways it is manifested have led many people to make erroneous judgments about what are the causes and what are the effects.

This is one case in which the cause of something complex is itself really simple. Inflation of our money is caused by the deficit spending policies of the Congress. When the government runs in the red, it simply prints additional money and bonds to cover its debt. This bogus "money" is pumped into the economy through the Federal Reserve, thus diminishing the value of the money already in circulation.

To make a homely analogy, consider a pot of soup. Add a gallon of water and you will have a lot more soup, but it will take a good many more bowls of it to make a nourishing meal.

Naturally there are other factors that aggravate inflation, but the conscious action of the government is at the root of it. Therefore it does little good to denounce the oil companies, the utility companies, or the supermarkets, as some people do when they write to me. We might as well blame inflation on sunspots or the configuration of the stars. None of these agencies has the right to print money and declare it legal tender.

And for sheer hypocrisy, nothing can beat the nerve of politicians who continually permit the government to spend beyond its means, and then blame the resulting inflation on the "greediness" of the citizens.

Inflating the currency is tantamount to theft. It is a form of embezzlement, a "covert operation" if there ever was one, and an immoral act. Inflation is destructive of free enterprise, since it discourages saving and the investment of capital. Who will save dollars that are certain to become worth less and less?

The limit of our federal indebtedness is supposed to be specified by law. But every year, as the list of federal programs lengthens and widens, the bills come in higher and higher; and so the Congress, which voted all these programs into existence in the first place, just routinely votes to extend the debt limit.

I recently stood on the Senate Floor and watched prominent senators, alleged to be experts in economics, conduct a solemn discussion of what level of indebtedness would be more "appropriate" — whether a $40 billion deficit would be more "appropriate" than $55 billion. I made the suggestion at the time that the word they should be using was not "appropriate" at all, but "appalling."

Until the days of the Great Society in the 1960s, we had at least one restraint on our money: part of our nation's currency had to be backed by gold or silver. Do you remember the days when dollar bills were "Silver

Certificates" and not "Federal Reserve Notes"? This very sensible and reasonable requirement thus kept down the amount of "funny money" in circulation.

But since that time, this requirement has been eliminated, and the printing presses can now be run all day and all night until the politicians have what they need. Our coinage, too, has suffered the same fate. You don't need to be a numismatist to know that a quarter or half dollar made of real silver is now worth far more than its face value. The old saying that what this country needs is a good five-cent nickel was right on the money.

When the public grows increasingly alarmed about the havoc inflation is wreaking in their households, they frequently demand — and rightfully so — that the Congress do something about it. And the Congress usually is quick to oblige by compounding the original crime: the members raise a great hue and cry for wage and price controls. When these are instituted, you have everything in place for shortages, recession, unemployment, and the rise of economic tyranny in the executive branch. If this sounds like a rerun of what we have just been through in the seventies, that is the scenario exactly.

Having once been down this blind alley, and having thus suffered the worst recession since the thirties (and the Great Depression, let us not forget, was also brought on by inflationary pressures promoted by government credit policies), we should now start laying the foundation for genuine and enduring prosperity by insisting on a return to "hard" money.

The government is morally obligated to maintain the soundness of the dollar as the sine qua non of the economic stability of the country. This derives from the commandment *Thou shalt not steal,* which applies as much to governments as to individuals.

Our people should insist, first of all, that the waste and extravagance endemic in the federal government be swiftly eliminated. In addition, the Congress must work to keep expenditures in line with tax revenues. Finally, we should reinstitute the backing of our money with precious metals.

These steps would have several highly beneficial results for all Americans. First, it would restore confidence in the dollar and stabilize its value. It would also impose a discipline on those in charge of appropriating public funds. Last, and most important, it would make our currency independent of political manipulation and chicanery. Money that is redeemable on demand is the greatest possible asset to a free people. The money will have an objective value no matter what party is in power.

Through the long and tedious years of Watergate, we heard over and over again the righteous pleas for taking money out of politics. I am all for doing that. I am also all for going one step further and *taking the politics out of our money*. Once we do that, we will have no need to fear the kind of inflation which, in our own time, paralyzed both Germany and China and delivered them over to totalitarian control.

Jesse meets with guest in his Washington office.

Dorothy and Jesse Helms in 1945.

Jesse submitted a bill to grant Alexander Solzhenitsyn honorary United States Citizenship.

Jesse after receiving award from Veterans of Foreign Wars, June 1977.

John Wayne is a member of the Friends for Jesse Club.

Senator Jim Allen (D. Ala.), Jesse, and Dr. Leo Jenkins, Chancellor of East Carolina University.

Jesse and Dot visit with Dr. and Mrs. Billy Graham.

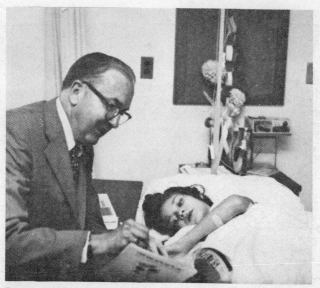

Jesse visiting with children at Cerebral Palsy hospital in Durham, N.C.

Jesse and Jim "Catfish" Hunter at reception in Edenton, N.C.

Jesse and North Carolina Governor Jim Hunt after purchase of $12 million of North Carolina tobacco by Chinese Trade Delegation. Jesse was instrumental in making arrangements for tobacco to be included in trade agreement.

Jesse and Jack Albertson chat with young lady at Duke Children's Benefit Golf Tournament.

Former U.S. Senator and long-time Congressman Alton Lennon (D. N.C.), Jesse, and Alan Shepard (America's first astronaut).

Jesse discusses attacks by HEW on North Carolina's tobacco industry.

Jesse and students from Western Carolina University in Sylva, N.C.

Richard Petty and Jesse in Washington

Mrs. Dorothy Helms

Senator Jesse Helms, right, and other key Senators fighting the Panama Canal giveaway confer with the representatives of the major veterans groups in Washington. Pictured seated: Sen. Bob Dole (R. Kansas), Sen. Orrin Hatch (R. Utah), Sen. Paul Laxalt (R. Nev.), Sen. Strom Thurmond (R. S.C.), Sen. Harry Byrd (I. Va.), Sen. James Allen (D. Ala.), and Helms.

Jesse takes time out to visit with high school student band.

U.S. Senator Harry F. Byrd Jr. (I. Va.) speaks for Jesse in Elizabeth City, N.C.

Jesse has worked extensively on behalf of handicapped children.

Jesse and University of Arkansas football coach Lou Holtz visit with students in Raleigh, N.C.

Jesse in his office during a moment away from the Senate floor.

Jesse "clogs" with youngsters in Asheville, N.C.

CHAPTER TEN

An Echo of Will Rogers

IT REALLY shouldn't surprise me, but somehow it always does, when I am reminded that most of today's young people never heard of Will Rogers.

Will Rogers and Wiley Post, as every old-timer recalls, died over forty years ago in a plane crash. Most people my age probably can describe their reaction the day they heard the news. I remember the sadness I felt. I was thirteen and a carrier boy for the *Charlotte News* in my little hometown of Monroe. It was a dreary afternoon as I delivered the sad news about Will Rogers and Wiley Post.

One day recently as I was returning to the Senate Chamber following a meeting on the House of Representatives side of the Capitol, I had a chance meeting with a group of young North Carolinians on a tour. It so happened that we met alongside the statue of Will Rogers which is positioned about one hundred feet from one of the entrances to the House Chamber. I explained to the tour group that this is the only statue facing the House Chamber — in keeping with his suggestion that "Somebody better keep an eye on that crowd."

There ought to be one facing the Senate Chamber as well. More Americans ought to keep their eyes on both houses of Congress.

63

Will Rogers delighted his millions of followers with his good-natured ridicule of Congress. He once observed that the liberties of the American people were not safe "as long as Congress is in session." How right he was!

He once remarked, "Never blame a legislative body for NOT doing something. When they do nothing, they don't hurt anybody. When they DO something is when they become dangerous. . . . Congress meets tomorrow morning. Let us pray to the Lord to give us strength to bear that which is about to be inflicted upon us. . . ."

The wisdom of Will Rogers is apparent to anyone who has followed the activities of Congress for the past three or four decades. Congress is responsible, in large measure, for the inflation now wreaking havoc on the American economy. It is Congress that has voted the enormous federal deficits that have saddled this country with a stupefying debt of far more than half a trillion dollars.

It is Congress, playing politics, that created the outrageous welfare programs that have encouraged citizens to stop working for a living. It is Congress that has permitted small businessmen to be swamped with federal regulations, controls, and time-consuming paperwork. It is Congress that has allowed the federal bureaucracy to double and treble, to the point that almost every American is frustrated with federal controls of almost every type.

It was a great loss to all of us, the day that Will Rogers died in that plane crash in 1935. Had he lived, he might have stood, in person, outside the halls of Congress — where his statue is standing now — and kept an eye on what was going on. He represents a wholesome skepticism of big government and fast-talking politicians that we need to revive today.

CHAPTER ELEVEN

The Right to Life

MANY THEORISTS have speculated on the nature and function of civil government. Western thinkers have been pondering this question since the days of Plato and Aristotle. Though the greatest philosophers may disagree on the arrangements of the state, their consensus has always been that the state exists, first of all, *to protect the lives of the citizens*.

That is why we have armies. That is why we have police departments. The protection of innocent lives has been a principle so ingrained in our thinking and traditions that in our own lifetimes we have expended thousands of lives and countless millions of dollars in bloody battles to defeat the armies of those nations — such as Nazi Germany under Hitler — who callously held a more expedient or utilitarian view of human life. It is a paradox, but it shows the depth of that conviction.

Few of those who were making the most grievous sacrifices for our country's efforts in 1943, for example, would have dreamed that, thirty years later, the Supreme Court would capitulate to the very kind of thinking that was fundamental to our enemies then.

On January 22, 1973, the Supreme Court struck down the state statutes prohibiting abortion. Despite some minor quibbles and qualifications appended to this decision, its effects were swift and wide ranging. Suddenly women found they had a new civil right — to dispose of their unborn children. And abortion — which civilized people from the days of Hammurabi to the present had looked upon as the vilest of crimes — overnight became respectable.

The medical profession, with a few noble and courageous exceptions, accepted the decision with the mildest of demurs. And soon the abortionist, hitherto regarded as the very dregs of humanity, was presiding over an immensely profitable obstetrical subspecialty and was celebrated as a benefactor of the community.

Since that decision, such a short time ago, our country has lost more lives through abortion than we have lost in all the wars and traffic accidents in our history. The toll in lives and human anguish has been utterly unprecedented and utterly appalling.

I am the author of a constitutional amendment to restore to unborn children the right of equal protection under the law. My efforts in this behalf have brought me in touch with every possible spectrum of opinion on this immensely divisive issue. Well-meaning friends have pointed out to me the political liabilities of the stand I have taken. I have been castigated by women's liberationists, editorialists, physicians, lawyers, and every kind of ad hoc group that can afford the price of postage.

I have a thick file of letters and articles containing every rationalization of abortion that the human mind can devise. Some of them are truly tragic situations, and no one could be unmoved after reading these accounts. If I had any inclination toward condoning situation ethics, this correspondence, in its volume and in its intensity, could probably confirm me in it.

But I oppose abortion because it is something God has forbidden to us. God's law condemns the taking of innocent life, and as a lawmaker myself, I must in conscience accept and observe the prior laws of God.

Whatever political penalties are exacted by this

stand I will gladly pay. As a believing Christian, I do not resort to the dodge of having one set of principles for public issues and another for my personal use. Politically speaking, I am content to share the convictions of Thomas Jefferson, who pointed out to King George that it is the Creator of mankind who confers upon us all the right to life, to liberty, and to the pursuit of happiness.

Now that the government has established that citizens at one end of the age spectrum are expendable for reasons of convenience and social policy, I fear for the other. I fear the day may come when the elderly, whom some similarly consider a burden on the resources of society, can look forward to some kind of federally sanctioned — and probably federally financed — program to terminate their lives. Indeed the ground is being prepared for this in the numerous death-with-dignity campaigns under way at the present time.

If one accepts the utilitarian view of life that inspired so much of the acceptance of abortion, euthanasia is the logical sequence. If we are willing to sacrifice the lives of those whose productive years are yet to come, what is to prevent us from cutting off the lives of those who can no longer pull their own weight in society? And more to the point, who will be around to defend our lives — yours and mine — some decades hence when we have just reared a generation of young people for whom abortion is as American as apple pie?

I am often struck by the accusation from proabortionists that their opponents are unfeeling and devoid of compassion when they object to "safe, legal abortions." It seems never to occur to these people that although a handful of black-robed justices can indeed decree abortion legal, according to their rights, not even the most expert surgeons can ever make it safe. Any abortion is fraught with danger for the mother, and it is 100 percent lethal to the baby. Indeed, that lethality is the purpose of an abortion. And it is a strange kind of compassion that exudes sympathy for the mother who wants to kill her child, and looks upon the helpless child as something to be exterminated.

It still astonishes many people that abortion — and what is even more widespread, the *toleration* of abortion — has so quickly become an accomplished fact in the U.S. Overnight it seems we went from a country where almost every state had laws prohibiting abortion, to one where almost all prohibitions were swept away. But it is important to realize that fifty years of relentless propagandizing, starting in Germany in the twenties, were necessary to prepare the scientific, medical, and legal groundwork for what goes on in our hospitals today. Though these efforts received a temporary setback from the bad publicity surrounding the extermination of so-called social undesirables in World War II, they resumed again in the fifties. After God was officially declared dead by the reigning experts in the sixties, scientific rationalism lost no time in taking over.

No one can read the future, but I should not be surprised if it takes many years to convince our people of the true horror and the moral repugnance of abortion. The true and lasting answer for unwanted pregnancy is not more and bigger abortion mills, and the physical and mental scars they inflict on those who patronize them, but rather a return to biblical teaching on sexual mores.

As Christians we must examine our own attitudes in a world growing ever more hostile to "unplanned," "unwanted" children. We must find ways to give of ourselves to see that the mothers of these children have an alternative to slaughtering them.

In the meantime, we must not lose sight of the anomaly, the odd spectacle, that now exists in our country — where there is strong agitation to make tough laws protecting wolves and where it is already a federal offense to destroy an eagle's egg and where all protection has been forfeited on unborn human life.

CHAPTER TWELVE

Justice and the Welfare State

CONSERVATIVES WHO fight against the expansion of more and more federal intrusions into our lives, and who struggle against the plundering of the federal treasury by the elected representatives of special interest groups, are frequently and falsely portrayed as being insensitive to need, to suffering, and to social inequity.

No one enjoys this kind of vilification. It is much more flattering to be hailed as a champion of the downtrodden — especially when this adulation is purchased with other people's money. That, I suppose, is why we have such lopsided liberal majorities in the Congress.

I recall an episode in the Senate sometime back when a well-known member was imploring his colleagues to be "generous" in appropriating money for a special interest group to which this member was particularly devoted. As I listened to his pleadings, thoughts of Davy Crockett came immediately to my mind.

The senator was explaining that the "few million dollars" he had in mind would not even be noticed in the total federal budget — which, of course, is precisely the argument advanced whenever Congress takes another step toward socialism. Thousands of little giveaways have become enormous giveaways. The spending practices of the federal government, as a result, long ago reached runaway proportions.

Thus Davy Crockett came to mind. Far more than a century ago, old Davy saw the danger in this kind of practice. He also recognized the immorality of it. Every schoolboy is familiar with Davy Crockett's career as an adventurer and explorer, and almost everyone is aware that Davy, at age forty-nine, was among the 186 men killed at the Alamo. Not so many know that he served for six years in the U.S. House of Representatives.

It's too bad that Congressman Crockett is not in Washington these days. He is needed here, as he was one day in the spring of 1830 when the House of Representatives hastily took up a proposal to appropriate some federal funds for the widow of a distinguished naval officer. Several eloquent speeches were made in support of the proposal, and it appeared that the bill would be approved by a wide margin. Just before the vote, however, Congressman Crockett arose.

"Mr. Speaker," he began, "I have as much respect for the memory of the deceased naval officer, and as much sympathy for the sufferings of the living — if suffering there be — as any man in this House of Representatives. But we must not permit our respect for the dead, or our sympathy for a part of the living, to lead us into an act of injustice to the *balance* of the living.

"I will not," Davy Crockett continued, "go into an argument to prove that Congress has no power to appropriate this money as an act of charity. Every member of this body *knows* that we do not. We have the right, as individuals, to give away as much of our *own money* as we please in charity, but as members of Congress we have no right to appropriate even one dollar of the public money [for such a purpose]. Some eloquent and beautiful appeals have been made to us upon the ground that this is a debt *due* the deceased."

Congressman Davy Crockett paused, looked around him, and then continued:

"Mr. Speaker, the deceased [naval officer] lived long after the close of the war; he was in office drawing his salary to the day of his death, and I have never heard that the government was in arrears to him."

His gaze fixed on his colleagues, Davy Crockett went on:

"Every man in this House of Representatives knows that [this] is not a debt. We cannot, without the grossest corruption, appropriate this money upon the pretense that it is the payment of a debt. We have not the semblance of Constitutional authority to appropriate it as a charity."

Then came the clincher. Davy said:

"Mr. Speaker, I have said we have the right to give as much money *of our own* as we please. I am the poorest man on this floor. I cannot vote for this bill, but I will give one week's pay to the object, and if every member of this Congress will do the same, it will amount to more money [for the lady] than the bill [proposed]."

Years later, Crockett contemplated that day in Congress. He told friends, "There is one thing now to which I will call your attention. You remember that I proposed to give a week's pay. There were in that House of Representatives many very wealthy men — men who think nothing of spending a week's pay or a dozen weeks' pay — for a dinner or a wine party when they have something personal to accomplish by it. Some of them made beautiful speeches about . . . so insignificant a sum as $10,000 — as long as the people were to pay it. . . . But not one of them responded to my proposition to put up their own money."

Matters haven't improved since Davy Crockett's day. They've just grown a lot worse. Hypocrisy is still masquerading as philanthropy in the halls of Congress. And the American people's money is being spent for some very strange things.

CHAPTER THIRTEEN

The Work-Less Ethic

I STILL HAVE not forgotten the tremors of alarm that rocked the Department of Health, Education and Welfare when word got out in Washington sometime ago that the number of welfare recipients throughout America had decreased by three-tenths of one percent during the preceding month.

It was something the bureaucrats had never anticipated, and great was their chagrin. The name of the welfare game, if you are a bureaucrat administering these programs, is more recipients, not fewer. During the past fourteen years, the number of citizens living on welfare has increased 500 percent.

And this has been the result of many and diverse derelictions: a Congress that appropriates money — billions of dollars of it annually — for purposes it neither understands nor even investigates; a federal bureaucracy obsessed with bigness and power; and state and local governments motivated by weakness or greed, or both, to try to outdo other states and communities in grabbing what they foolishly regard as "free money from Washington" and mistakenly call "federal aid."

In an effort that is proving disastrously successful, the federal government is rapidly moving to make state and local governments the merest vassals of its power.

The most effective means of whipping them into line has been through a process called "matching funds." The federal bureaucracy, for example, dreams up new welfare schemes that no state or local government would willingly accept under normal circumstances. But the bureaucracy baits the trap! It offers "free" millions in federal funds to states and local governments who in turn agree to put up some of their own tax funds in order to receive the so-called federal aid.

From that point on, Big Daddy takes over. Federal officials make the rules; federal agents make certain that the projects are operated as they dictate, and never mind how much hostility and frustration may be generated at the local level.

Some years ago I served as a city councilman myself, and I know how tough it is to hold out against the tempting argument that "if we don't get ours, somebody else will." This is the booby trap that too many local officials have been falling into for far too long. It is precisely the position that those who advocate a centralization of power and control in Washington want local officials to take. For what the federal government finances, the federal government controls. Furthermore, what the federal government finances, the people back home pay for through their taxes.

The federal government has no orchard of money trees in Washington. It can give nothing that it does not first take from the people, and then only after knocking off a walloping carrying charge from every dollar that comes through its hands.

The irony in all this, of course, is that the federal government — which has no money to "share," since it is already burdened with an astronomical debt — is acting the role of every unregenerate debauchee in luring local governments into the same spendthrift habits that may well undo the country.

HEW bureaucrats are not the only folks in Washington interested in setting up a leisure class, subsidized by the labors of their countrymen. The Congress, which duly responds to the pressures of organized labor, regularly pushes up the legal minimum wage, thereby forcing employers to dismiss many individuals whose services they cannot afford at that rate of pay.

Naturally this has many social consequences. For example, neighbors of ours consider themselves lucky if they can find high-school boys willing to mow their lawns for any price. While driving from my home in Raleigh to the airport one day recently, I counted thirty-six boys doing nothing. There was one cluster, eight or ten, standing in front of a neighborhood drugstore. A pool hall at one corner had five or six outside, and heaven knows how many inside. Three automotiles, each bearing three or more teen-agers, roared past as I continued toward the Durham highway and the airport. And so it went. I recall seeing one boy — just one — behind a mower. But I also saw three elderly men doing yard work.

"So what?" you may ask. Maybe a whole lot. Perhaps this little piece of imprecise sociological research points up a lot of ailments that agonize the country just now: the drug craze, the crime, and even the celebrated breakdown in communication between the older and the younger generations.

It is possible that our luxuriously brought-up youngsters are gathering together for love-ins and bugouts, not because they can't find anything to do, but because, generally speaking, they don't want to find it, and they don't have to find it. And the people who might otherwise hire them are doubly confounded — by a government that puts artificial restrictions on them, and by an attitude of indifference to work and accomplishment.

Necessity is the mother of a lot of things, not the least of which is incentive. That, after all, is human nature's response, and until fairly recent times, this caused human beings to get off their backsides and look for ways to make a contribution to the world. One thing is certain: a fellow who has a demanding job — unless he is a liberal in the government — has neither the time nor the inclination to join mobs and movements dedicated to the destruction of his country. If he is a radical leftist who collects a government paycheck — well, that's a different story.

CHAPTER FOURTEEN

The Santa Claus Syndrome

DURING THE several days just prior to shutting down for Christmas, some sessions ago, the Congress was debating almost everything under the sun. It was year-end-clearance time. Altogether it was scarcely more than a great surge of sound and fury signifying nothing — except, perhaps, the ineptness of most of those chosen to operate the country's legislative system.

In recent years there has been a rising tide of criticism of "the system." The criticism, for the most part, has been neither fair nor valid. The system is excellent; the primary fault lies with politicians and legislators and bureaucrats and judges in high places who have manhandled, not only the system, but the very meaning of freedom itself. As a consequence, the future of the country, as long as they are in charge of it, is depressingly bleak.

Every man is a philosopher when he pauses to contemplate the travail of his time. But too often the philosophy is a contradiction of reality. It happened in the Senate of the United States the Monday before Christmas. One of the issues at hand at the moment was a proposal to guarantee every man an annual income, *whether or not he is willing to work for it.* One prominent liberal senator is an across-the-board advocate of all welfare programs. It is good politics in his state to promise something for nothing — the trick is to put an acceptable face on it. A man in public office needs to sound compassionate, you see, when he is proposing to give away other people's money.

So the senator, who is now a millionaire, told his fellow senators about the depression days of his youth, the days of the WPA. His mother, he said, got a $90-a-month job as a violinist in a symphony orchestra and was paid by the federal government for working eight hours a day. The senator spoke of dignity and self-respect and how much the job meant to his family.

A poignant story and a good point — except that it offers very little support for the senator's advocacy of the proposition that people *today* ought to be paid for *not* working.

Back in the 1930s a lot of folks made a lot of well-justified jokes about the WPA. Critics of President Roosevelt often lampooned him for the WPA concept. But this much can be said for FDR: he regarded and described his various welfare programs *as welfare*. Moreover, he intended — or said he intended — that they be temporary in nature. The concept seemed clear that able-bodied citizens needing assistance were to be given it in the form of a job, even if a menial one. In any case, it was required that the able-bodied perform some kind of labor to qualify for a government check.

The fact that the WPA quickly became an almost comical political boondoggle served to emphasize that the greater and broader a government welfare program becomes, the more susceptible to corruption it becomes. The outrageous disclosures of fraud and thievery growing out of the "poverty" programs in more recent years supply ample evidence that human nature does not change.

Yet all this should not be taken to mean that human suffering and need can be justifiably ignored by the more fortunate. To the contrary, if Americans hope to reverse the self-defeating and inequitable burden of political welfare programs, they must take a look at their own stewardship in personal humanitarianism and compassion. This has become a lost concept in our time. Charity, which once began at home and in the heart, has been taken over by the government and has been transformed into a well-calibrated political mechanism that cares less for humanity than for votes in the next election.

It was ironic, in a way, that this subject was being discussed in the Congress at the beginning of Christmas week. The One whose birthday was to be observed a few days later was not mentioned once during the debate. Nor were mentioned any of the admonitions that Christ voiced about how man is to fulfill his personal responsibilities.

Nowhere at any time did Christ mention a government welfare program, let alone endorse one. He suggested another way, one that would work. But neither the politicians nor the people have paid much attention. They have preferred instead to try to do it *their* way. Thus the more millions they appropriate, and the more burdens they lay on the shoulders of our productive citizens, denying them the means to take care of their own needs, the more demand they will create for federal doles of every conceivable kind.

CHAPTER FIFTEEN

A Second Look at Foreign Aid

WITHOUT A doubt, the greatest racket of all time is the rip-off of the American taxpayers in the name of foreign aid. At times I take comfort in the fact that since coming to the Senate I have not voted to send one dime overseas for these programs. Moreover, I have been zealous to see, in these times of recession and economic hardship at home, that the American people are told the full truth about the extent of their involuntary philanthropies abroad.

During the last thirty years, foreign aid has cost the taxpayers of this country $172 billion. Coincidentally our federal debt during this period increased by $384 billion. Thus foreign aid was equivalent to 44 percent of our national debt. For one year alone, the interest on the amount that our government had to borrow in order to give away costs the taxpayers of the United States $9.25 billion.

Let us face this truth: We are not sending our super-fluous bounty abroad; we are mortgaging ourselves into eternity for these giveaways.

Probably the most outstanding characteristic of the American people historically has been its magnanimity and generosity to those afflicted by famine, disaster, and want. The specter of the starving multitudes in Africa and

Asia has time and time again prompted an outpouring of humanitarian relief from the people of this country.

But I am talking about something else — about the exploitation of this generosity by the politicians of one country for the benefit of their opposite numbers in other countries.

The really stupendous cover-up of modern times is not Watergate at all, but the vast sums of money this country has exported overseas. The keys to Fort Knox have been delivered to foreign countries, many of which could not be considered "underdeveloped" by any stretch of the imagination.

Consider, for example, West Germany, which has received $4.9 billion; France, which has received $8.2 billion; and Japan, the recipient of $3.8 billion. All of this, mind you, since World War II.

For many years there really was no way of knowing the true extent of our commitments overseas. Before 1971, foreign-aid figures were carefully dispersed through the budgets of many departments and agencies. Since that time, the Congress has required that all foreign-aid amounts be published annually in one place, and the result has been a truly eye-popping accounting.

I think it is time for a sober reassessment of what this hemorrhage of dollars has accomplished. Hundreds of nations now hold these dollars, and it is nothing but crocodile tears when our public officials bewail the unfavorable balance of payments ratio at the same time they countenance these shipments of money abroad.

The recent recession has pointed up the tremendous capital shortage facing American industry. Many businesses are unable to raise the money they need to expand or modernize their operations, with a resulting loss of jobs. Public works projects like airports, harbors, and the like may be stalled in this country because of lack of funds, but highways, dams, schools, and transportation facilities undertaken overseas with U.S. aid funds always go on as planned. Five years ago it was estimated that of the 3½ billion people then in the world, all but 36 million had received aid from the United States.

For the same reasons why we should avoid setting up the welfare state at home, we should avoid setting up the welfare world abroad. A good many of the starry-eyed liberals running our foreign policy will come before the Congress and maintain that the best way to avoid communist takeovers in so-called underdeveloped countries is to finance socialism. Socialism, they insist, will somehow vaccinate these countries against communism. That's horsefeathers.

There was a time when this country, too, was underdeveloped. The way it developed was through the operation of free enterprise and the market economy. The U.S. does not hold any patent on this process. It still works, for any country that will seriously undertake to use it.

Government aid works, in the long run, to the detriment of those countries accepting it. Like all welfare, it kills the incentive to produce and become self-sufficient. It stifles development, rather than promoting it, and thus creates the "need" for more and more aid. Naturally this pleases the bureaucrats who draw up the plans and estimates. And then, as aid becomes a way of life, recipient nations find that by plotting an ever-more-leftward course, they can quietly blackmail Uncle Sam into raising the stakes. This is such an old story now that anyone who thinks we are going to reap any harvest of gratitude and cooperation from these client states is hopelessly naive.

The harsh truth is, there are many countries in the world that are materially very badly off. It is our duty to help them. The way to help them is to share with them our political philosophy and our expertise and to encourage private investment there. This is how our country profited from Europe.

It seems to me that if a case is to be made at all for continuing any kind of foreign aid, the way I read the red ink, the United States should be getting aid, not giving it away.

CHAPTER SIXTEEN

Bad Debts

IT WOULD BE bad enough if foreign aid consisted simply of cash handouts for which the Congress could be held responsible. But foreign aid takes many forms, and the executive branch is not without its own practitioners of the art.

I realize that it is impossible for the news media to cover everything that goes on in government. But I often find myself wishing there could be a shift in emphasis — at least to the extent that the American people can be made aware of what is being done with their money.

I wonder, for example, what the public reaction would have been had the taxpayers been informed that, during the past three years, the U.S. State Department wiped out more than $5 billion owed by foreign governments to the United States?

To be precise, Henry Kissinger and his associates settled several enormous debts for about two cents on the dollar. The foreign governments involved in the "settlements" owed us, as I say, more than $5 billion: they paid us $112 million. The President, on the recommendation of the Secretary of State, *canceled* the remainder of the debt.

The Communists of the Soviet Union were the largest beneficiaries of this generosity. The State Department agreed to cancel $2.6 billion in claims arising from the Soviet Union's lend-lease indebtedness to the United States in World War II. The Soviets settled that $2.6 billion debt for — would you believe — $48 million!

Then there is India, which is making no attempt to disguise its true identity as an oppressive dictatorship. That nation is surely no friend to the United States. A debt of $2.2 billion, owed to us by India, was cancelled. India still owes the U.S. about $3 billion in other debts: no doubt that will be "forgiven," also, in years to come.

These and other debts owed to the United States have been canceled by Secretary of State Kissinger by the simple expedient of recommendation to the President. At long last, however, the Senate voted recently to prohibit such "settlements" unless approved by the Congress.

I can think of no better example of using your right hand to cut off your left than the instance of U.S. aid to India. We provide financial assistance of every kind to India — a subsidy of hundreds of millions of dollars — yet India has repudiated everything that freedom signifies. Democracy does not exist in India. This is but another example of U.S. diplomacy in which we foolishly try to "buy" friends. It can't be done.

We know there is hunger in India. We also know that India has diverted hundreds of millions of dollars of the aid we sent to that government. Diverted it where?

On May 9, 1974, India detonated her first nuclear device, the development of which cost an immense sum by the economical standards of any country. This was money that India could have spent improving its agricultural system so that millions of hungry people could eat.

In November 1975, I submitted an amendment to the Senate to cut off further U.S. aid to India unless and until India agrees to stop spending enormous sums of money on the development of nuclear bombs. Senator Hubert Humphrey spoke against my amendment for forty-five minutes, never quite addressing himself to the issue.

There were no more than five senators in the chamber during the debate. As I expected, my amendment was defeated — but my point had been made. It showed that the "liberals" in the Senate will vote to give away the American taxpayers' money all over the world, even to hostile countries, without even bothering to listen to debate on the matter.

We need look no further to understand why the federal government is now in debt for more than half a trillion dollars.

CHAPTER SEVENTEEN

Another Kind of Giveaway

IN WATCHING the careers of the leading lights of the Department of State — specifically Secretary Kissinger and Ambassador Ellsworth Bunker, who brought us Peace With Honor in Vietnam — I think nothing describes their activities better than a paraphrase of Churchill: Never have so few given away so much belonging to so many.

The proposed giveaway of the Panama Canal has become front-page news, thanks to the determined efforts of Governor Reagan. Few Americans are aware that the U.S. government would have signed away its rights to the Canal Zone years ago, had it not been for the resolute opposition of a handful of citizens and members of Congress who were well aware that the loss of this canal, no matter how protracted the timetable, would be an immense blow to the United States and to the defense of freedom in this hemisphere. It is also the best gift we could confer on Fidel Castro.

Americans should bear in mind that the people of the United States bought and paid for the Panama Canal. It was built with funds provided by the American taxpayers and constructed by the engineering genius of our people. We have managed it to the great advantage of all the maritime nations of the world. The property is ours, by treaty and by purchase, and a treaty can be broken or changed only by the Senate and the Congress of the United States. Even then, it requires a two-thirds vote.

The treaty between the United States and the Republic of Panama was signed on November 18, 1903. It was officially proclaimed on February 26, 1904. There is not the slightest possibility that the U.S. Senate would vote, by the required two-thirds majority, to surrender this country's ownership of the Panama Canal. So Mr. Kissinger has resorted to maneuvering in the background to bypass the will of the Senate.

The Kissinger strategy is to use what I consider unconstitutional means to erode the 1903 treaty and thereby virtually give away the Panama Canal. In 1974, Mr. Kissinger signed an "agreement" with the Republic of Panama which stipulated that "the Panamanian territory in which the Canal is situated shall be returned to the jurisdiction of the Republic of Panama." But the canal is not situated in Panamanian territory.

Specifically what the Secretary had in mind was to give the Panamanian government control of police and fire protection in the Canal Zone, plus control of the postal service.

Secretary Kissinger has no authority to enter into any such agreement — but he did it, nonetheless, and in the name of the President of the United States. Unfortunately the President has as yet been unwilling to reject this arrogant act by his Secretary of State. I hope that the President may change his mind, after examining article IV, section 3 of the Constitution of the United States, which declares:

"The Congress shall have Power to dispose of and make all needful Rules and Regulations respecting the Territory or other Property belonging to the United States."

The intent of the Constitution is clear: *Congress* has "the Power" — not the President or the Secretary of State — "to dispose of" the Panama Canal.

This is another instance when the Congress needs to face up to its responsibility and exercise its authority. That can best be done, in the case of the proposed giveaway of the Panama Canal, by telling the President and Secretary Kissinger that the canal is U.S. property, and that neither the President nor the Secretary should attempt to contravene the law and the Constitution.

CHAPTER EIGHTEEN

Ropes to the Hangman

No GENERATION of Americans has been called upon to make as many sacrifices on behalf of freedom in the world as we who are living now. Since the start of the twentieth century, we have been called upon to fight four ferocious wars. From the Atlantic to the farthest reaches of the Pacific we have struggled heroically to overcome the forces inimical to freedom. Never have we had a generation so inured to hardship and sacrifice, when they were called for, and never have we had a generation of politicians who were so adept at throwing away the fruits of our victories.

War is the ultimate sanction. Wars and armies are not the handmaids of the diplomats. The great mistake made by President Truman was his refusing to allow our army to press for victory in Korea, preferring to permit the carnage to go on while long and pointless negotiations dragged on with the Communists. For years the talks continued, and to this day nothing has been accomplished in Korea except perpetuation of the status quo.

Moreover, our failure to defeat the Communists decisively in Korea permitted them to solidify their position in China and thereafter to export revolution to the countries of Southeast Asia.

Presidents Johnson and Nixon both persevered in

the same naive faith in "negotiation," disregarding the advice of their highest military advisers.

As the years went by and the bloodshed continued unabated, the bankruptcy of our policy became evident, and the American people began to challenge the very basis on which the war was waged.

Eight years after it began, the second war in which Americans were committed to the field and denied the option of victory came to its tragic conclusion. The Vietnam conflict had cost the lives of 56,000 of our fighting men, handicapped another 300,000, and devoured untold billions of tax dollars. In the end, we forced an ignoble and unworkable "truce" on our allies, the South Vietnamese, and we began a steady retreat from confrontation with the Soviet Union which continues to this day.

The Soviet Union had parlayed a modest investment in North Vietnam to conquer a huge, fertile, and mineral-rich peninsula strategically located at the crossroads of Asia. The Soviets did this by exploiting the fears of American politicians about the possibility of nuclear war.

Such a war, the Soviets well know, is unthinkable to Western politicians. But it is not unthinkable to the strategists in the Kremlin. Indeed, their whole outlook is predicated on war, and they think about it all the time.

The great war-weariness which the Americans felt in the late 1960s is a recurring phenomenon in world history. It had a counterpart in classical mythology when the Trojan people, their nerves and endurance worn down from holding off a protracted siege by the Greeks, were persuaded to open the gates and permit the entry of the great wooden horse that proved their undoing. America, too, on the advice of its own soothsayers, the commentators, joyfully greeted President Nixon's policy of detente. This, they were led to believe, would usher in a new era of peace and prosperity and dispel the "tensions" of the cold war.

Subsequent events have proved detente to be a horrendous adventure in self-delusion. Even as the battle raged in Vietnam, American liberals, in a display of credulity that has no equal in modern history, were swallowing the story that the Soviet Union wanted nothing more than to relax tensions in the world, to beat its swords into plowshares, and to devote its gargantuan energies solely to improving consumer goods for Soviet citizens.

The chief author of this deception in the United States was Henry Kissinger, President Nixon's National Security Adviser and later Secretary of State.

This was the same man who, while attending the Moscow Summit in 1974, turned to the reporters assigned to the event and said, "One of the things we have to ask ourselves as a country is what in the name of God is strategic superiority? What is the significance of it — politically, militarily, operationally — at these levels of numbers? What do you do with it?"

By that time it was late in the day to ask such a question, because two years earlier he had effectively wiped out any possibility of American superiority in the notorious SALT I agreement. The terms of this pact permitted the Soviets three nuclear missiles for every two the U.S. had, plus $1 billion worth of American grain, on credit, generously subsidized by the U.S. taxpayers.

Detente perhaps came to full flower in 1975, when the Soviets showed their pacific intentions by swallowing up six countries as the flow of American grain, heavy equipment, sophisticated technology (such as computers), and trade credits continued unabated to Moscow. In July of that year, President Ford revealed some of the more social aspects of detente when he refused to receive Alexsandr Solzhenitsyn at the White House, out of deference to the wishes of Comrade Brezhnev.

Of course, Mr. Solzhenitsyn in a recent speech had excoriated the willingness of American government and business leaders to abandon all moral restraints in their headlong pursuit of a mythical harvest of profits to be reaped from trade with the Soviets. Thus he denounced their gullibility and their greed in consummating deals which did nothing but strengthen the hands of the power elite in the Kremlin. Selling ropes to the hangman, he called it, and great was the displeasure of the Washington establishment.

Wherever he went, Mr. Solzhenitsyn, by virtue of his genius and courage, exposed the fraudulent nature of Mr. Kissinger's detente. When he spoke, he stirred something deep in the American spirit. Large numbers of people emerged from a dream world to perceive the unparalleled, unprecedented dangers to the West.

"World War III is over, and the West has lost it," Mr. Solzhenitzyn announced, and day by day the headlines bore him out as Portugal, Italy, and Angola were convulsed by political agitation. Western governments, sunk in torpor and apathy, were acquiescing in the conquest of one country after another, feeding the sharks in the hope that they would be eaten last.

Not all Americans, however, had fallen for this phony detente. Numerous other voices began to tell us of the magnitude of the formidable Soviet war machine which by 1975 had equaled or surpassed us in every category of military hardware except helicopters.

Foremost among these was Mr. Kissinger's nemesis, the Secretary of Defense, James R. Schlesinger. Secretary Schlesinger warned his disbelieving countrymen of the corrupting effect of their own weakness, a weakness measurable in armaments and preparedness, but even more devastating as a weakness of will.

"The gravest problem for the Western World," he declared, "is without question the loss of vision, of moral stamina, of national purpose." He assailed the liberal notion that our failure in Vietnam was the result of an excess of power — an absurd proposition, since we lost in Vietnam because we never used the power that we had. Needless to say, Mr. Schlesinger no longer is Secretary of Defense. There is little job security in leveling with the American people.

For more than thirty years the threat of nuclear war

has hung over the world. In spite of this, until detente the United States and its allies in the West stood, in Solzhenitsyn's phrase, "like granite" — and there was no nuclear war. The nuclear superiority of the United States, and not detente, prevented war.

The price of peace and survival is strength and overwhelming superiority, and this the Soviets well know. Of course they are eager to sign any kind of agreement proposed to stop the arms race; and while the West pathetically trusts in such scraps of paper, the Soviets never scruple about violating them. For decades the Soviets had worked unceasingly to attain nuclear and tactical parity with the United States. They were never able to get it until the United States voluntarily cut back its defenses. A policy which any sane man would look upon as suicide was hailed by the liberal pundits as a master stroke of genius.

The second tactical error of Mr. Kissinger's detente consists in its massive effort to redeem the hopeless failures of the Soviet economy. The Soviets' technology is spectacularly inefficient and incompetent. Their economy, harnessed to grandiose ambitions of conquering the world, is incapable of feeding their own citizens. Our strategy should be to exploit these weaknesses, not to rush in with the most advanced American equipment and millions of tons of grain to remove these pressures from the Kremlin bosses.

American leaders have been totally inept at using this country's leverage as the world's greatest producer of food. We should be exacting tough concessions from the Soviets in exchange for our grain. The disastrous crop failures on the collective farms over the last few years, and the reversion of whole regions in the Soviet Union to permafrost, have made the Soviets extremely vulnerable in this regard. But the United States has never pressed — and perhaps never even recognized — the advantage we have over them. Instead the Administration, by routinely contracting sales of millions of tons of grain, forfeited this advantage . . . and the Soviets proceeded full steam ahead to arrange for the Cubans to invade Angola.

Unless we have a swift reversal of these policies of drift and concession, not only will the tenure of this country as a great world power be one of the shortest in all history, but we will inevitably be reduced to a client state of the prospective world-wide Soviet Empire. Though many Americans prefer not to believe this possibility, only two alternatives confront us. We might prefer to put off action and decision, seeking but to live and let live and get on with our daily affairs.

Considering the might of our enemy, delaying action is not a reasonable option. Our forebears had the sense to heed the words of Paul Revere: "The British are coming!" Unless we heed the words of his counterparts today, of Schlesinger and Solzhenitsyn and a host of lesser prophets, we are going to be invaded: "The Russians are coming!" The possibility we refused to admit will come to pass, and we will be powerless to respond to it.

The moment of truth will have come upon us, and the agony and upheavel and desolation which we observed in the fall of Vietnam will be simply a foreshadowing of what to expect when the United States becomes the last of the falling dominoes.

Early in the 1800s, long before this country had any pretensions to great naval or military power, our ships were being harassed on the high seas by cutthroat bandits from the Barbary States. A young naval commander, confronted with the extortionate demands of a pirate chief, gave him an answer that should be ringing through the halls of Congress today. "Millions for defense," retorted Stephen Decatur, "but not one cent for tribute!"

As countries East and West continue to fall before Soviet aggression, thus exposing the criminal fraudulence of this policy of detente, I think we ought to bank our survival on the philosophy of Decatur and scrap the proven failures of Kissinger's detente, in fact as well as in name.

CHAPTER NINETEEN

A School Bus to Equality

"IDEOLOGY" IS a strange word coined at the time of the French Revolution to describe the common beliefs of the intellectuals who programed France into that upheaval. Whereas the United States fought its War for Independence to preserve the traditional rights of Englishmen, and thereafter set up a government firmly based on English law and custom, the liberal intellectuals in France wanted a complete break with their country's feudal past. So they had to invent a whole new party platform, you might say, spelling out their beliefs and their program for establishing a utopia where none had been before.

The shorthand for this ideology was the slogan "Liberty, Equality, and Fraternity." Liberty and fraternity, as events worked out, got short shrift. But the leftist notion of equality has continued to be the chief component of liberal ideology since the storming of the Bastille.

The Declaration of Independence indeed declares that all men are created equal. This particular phrase has been invoked over and over to justify programs completely alien to its original meaning. In the context in which Jefferson wrote, he was stressing that the citizens of the colonies shared an equal footing before the law with those who were living in England. Jefferson was emphatically not prescribing an economic or a moral equality to be established by the state.

The concept of equality as a mowing down of every person to a mass man has been a pitiably corrosive force in modern history. It has dominated the thinking of the Supreme Court over the last thirty years, with the result that a new class of bureaucrats has been established to superintend the arrangements of this completely artificial "equality."

Reasonable people know that equality, an abstract term, is a concept that applies to mathematics and only by analogy to human affairs. But this truth has never dawned on liberal intellectuals.

The most destructive application of this fanatical pursuit of "equality" is the insistence of the federal courts on "racial balance" in the public schools. Nowhere in the Constitution will you find any justification for what we have witnessed over the past few years: the forcible removal of young children from their neighborhood schools to fill quotas elsewhere that are decreed by the social engineers employed by the federal government.

The sight of their children being escorted many miles from their homes by police motorcades has jolted many parents into recognizing that regardless of what plans they had for their children's education, the government has plans of its own.

In the collision between parents' rights and liberal doctrine, the courts predictably came down heavily on the side of ideology. Parental reaction, of course, was hostile and unyielding. For years it was dismissed by politicians of both major parties with appalling smugness. When resentment of the busing edicts in Boston, Detroit, St. Louis, and other cities across the land reached a high rolling boil, it became obvious that the wishes of parents could be ignored only to the detriment of the nation and at the peril of the very survival of the public schools.

It was not until late 1975 that the Congress finally demonstrated an awareness that it can no longer disregard the will of the people — and the danger of violence arising from the continued defiance of the will of the people. Only then, for the first time, did a majority go on record as opposed to forced busing. This was a major breakthrough for those of us who are dedicated to bringing about a legislative reversal of the arbitrary decrees of HEW bureaucrats.

The doctrine that the end justifies the means is fundamental to the thinking of people committed to revolution. It seems to be an article of faith with the educational establishment. What does it matter if a generation of children is sacrificed, if educations are disrupted and neighborhoods inflamed, as long as somewhere over the rainbow we will achieve "equality"?

The edicts on forced busing treat human beings as if they were robots or the components of some kind of machine. They treat children and parents as if they were not emotional beings. Nevertheless, if human beings were not emotional, there would be no parents and no children. The concern that a man — even a bad man — feels for his children is probably the deepest and most altruistic feeling of which normal human beings are capable. And the concern he feels is the concern as he himself sees it — not as seen by some writer or bureaucrat who lives a thousand miles away, nor as someone of a different religion or cultural background, even though he may live next door, may see it.

It is possible that those who have enacted these regulations acted in the belief that they were guided by idealistic considerations. But it is foolishness to think that those parents who now resist busing, and who will surely continue to resist it, will ever be persuaded that an attitude which is an inseparable part of their love for their children should yield to someone else's dictatorial schemes. They will never come to feel guilty for what they think or for what they are doing. They will never listen to those who think that a parent cannot judge what is good for his child, or that he does not have a right to do so.

Indeed, why should they?

The *New York Times* has told us that these parents are wrong, that they must change, and that busing will solve a host of social problems. I use the name of that newspaper as a symbol for the particular mentality — clearly remote from that of most Americans — which has devised this form of cultural imperialism, so filled with contempt for the ordinary parent. At the same time, the news columns of that paper, despite the filter of liberal reporting, continually show us how miserable and irrational some of the policies advocated on its editorial page really are.

The battle against forced busing is really a battle for self-determination. Parents have the right to choose the environment they want for children, as long as they have the means to support it. And just as the parent determines what he wants for his child, so do the multitude of parents, who group themselves in neighborhoods and communities based on historic traditions, have the right to determine what kind of culture will be the setting for the education of their children. This is the heart of the matter.

CHAPTER TWENTY

Fourth of July

As I WRITE, there is scarcely a community across the country that has not been deeply involved in its own plans for celebrating our country's bicentennial. In Washington a record number of tourists are said to be coming to view the Capitol, the museums, and the various shrines and monuments that celebrate the epic achievements of a nation born free.

I sometimes wonder whether we run the risk, in all this rush and pageantry, of missing the point of what was really signified by the actions initiated in Independence Hall on that hot July day two centuries ago.

Mostly I sometimes wonder if July 4 isn't just deteriorating into one big costume party, or just another day off from work for most Americans.

All the same, July 4 has ever been a time of warm personal reminiscences for me. On that date my mind never fails to return to the days when I was a boy in Monroe, North Carolina. I remember the splendid celebrations — the parade down Main Street, the speeches on Court House Square, the fireworks, the prancing horses, the festive atmosphere that prevailed. Papa drove the town's only hook and ladder, and it was a time when all the children were allowed — no, encouraged — to climb aboard that magnificent red, shining vehicle for what now, more than four decades later, I remember as a very favorite sentimental journey through town.

There was one special July 4 that burned its way indelibly into my consciousness. That year the merchants got together for a big sales promotion and purchased an automobile that was to be given away at noon on Independence Day in a special ceremony at the court house.

Each merchant distributed tickets, and the stubs were deposited in a great container. During the weeks of the sales promotion prior to the big day, everyone collected and preserved numerous ticket stubs. I recall that Papa gave each of us three stubs that he had acquired when making purchases.

"Keep them," he said, "but don't count on getting an automobile for nothing." (I don't know what an eight-year-old boy would have done with a car, even if he had won it.)

That was one of the few times that I doubted Papa's advice. I kept those stubs and examined them so often that they were almost tattered. I slept with them under my pillow. I knew that Papa just had to be wrong this time: surely fortune would smile on me.

It didn't, of course. Someone else won the car. But I got something decidedly more valuable. I had a heart-to-heart talk with an understanding father who realized my deep disappointment.

In that talk he taught me that the way to achieve, the way to acquire something that I really wanted, was to work for it. Earn it, he said in his gentle way. He told me that in America people who work hard and save can do amazing things.

"Someday," Papa said, "you'll have a car — but it will be because you *earned* the money, not because you happened to hold a lucky ticket stub."

Looking back on it, I am glad I didn't win that automobile. If I had, I might never have had that heart-to-heart talk with my father. That episode, in the most effective sort of way, was the beginning of a little boy's understanding of the free enterprise system.

America never promises anybody happiness — only the *pursuit* of happiness, whether it manifests itself in the ownership of an automobile or a home or in any one of a thousand other ways. The genius of America is not in *winning* something or in being *given* it. The miracle of America is the opportunity to strive and work and *earn* the things we really want.

CHAPTER TWENTY-ONE

School Prayer

WHICH CAME first, one is prompted to inquire, the wholesale breakdown of moral values in our society, or the collapse of these values in the schools? What has been responsible for the maturing of a generation who reject the values and discipline and moral standards that Jews and Christians have respected and preserved for thousands of years?

Could the banishment of prayer and Bible reading from the public schools by order of the Supreme Court have had something to do with it?

In 1962, the Court held in *Engel* v. *Vitale* that the constitutional prohibition against governmental establishment of religion was violated by the recital of a non-denominational prayer at the beginning of each public school day. This same prayer, we should note, was written to try to preserve the right to pray, in order to meet the nonsectarian standards demanded by representatives of the so-called American Civil Liberties Union.

So it wasn't the "official" prayer that this group and their partisans on the bench were against — it was prayer, period. And promptly after this decision came the proscription of Bible readings, the observance of Christmas, and the singing of "America."

Thus we forfeited by judicial fiat the rights of millions

of American schoolchildren to invoke the blessings of God on their work. A handful of determined atheists and agnostics, in collaboration with a handful of Pharisees on the Supreme Court, succeeded in their great aim of using the power of the law to eradicate all mention of God and His Word in every public school classroom in America. And all this was accomplished in the name of civil liberties.

A greater crime against our children could hardly be conceived. In this case, as in so many others, the Court forced from the Constitution exactly the opposite conclusion from what the founding fathers intended. It escaped the Court's notice that this entire country was colonized by individuals seeking free expression of their religious beliefs. The Constitution prohibited the establishment of a religion by the Congress so that the right of freedom of religion would never be threatened.

It is hardly coincidence that the banishment of the Lord from the public schools has resulted in their being taken over by a totally secularist philosophy. Christianity has been driven out. In its place has been enshrined a permissiveness in which the drug culture has flourished, as have pornography, crime, and fornication — in short, everything but disciplined learning. This is the bitter fruit of the new civil right enunciated by our highest court: freedom *from* religion.

I think there is no more pressing duty facing the Congress than to restore the true spirit of the First Amendment. That is why I have worked hard on behalf of legislation which would permit the recitation of voluntary, nondenominational prayers in the public schools.

Fortunately the Constitution provides this alternative under the system of checks and balances. In anticipation of judicial usurpations of power, the framers of our Constitution wisely gave the Congress the authority, by a simple majority of both Houses, to check the Supreme Court by means of regulation of its appellate jurisdiction. Section 2 of article III states in clear and unequivocal language that the appellate jurisdiction of the Court is subject to "such Exceptions, and under such Regulations as the Congress shall make."

Thus my school prayer bill states simply that the federal courts shall not have jurisdiction to enter any judgment, decree, or order denying or restricting, as unconstitutional, voluntary prayer in any public school. Implicit in this bill is the understanding that the American citizen will have recourse to a judicial settlement of his rights, but this settlement will be made in the state courts of this nation and not in the federal courts. This is where our religious freedoms were always safeguarded for 173 years until they were nationalized by the Supreme Court.

The limited and specific objective of this bill, then, is to restore to the American people the fundamental right of voluntary prayer in the public schools. I stress the word *voluntary*. No individual should be forced to participate in a religious exercise that is contrary to his religious convictions, and the bill recognizes this important freedom. At the same time, the bill seeks to promote the free exercise by allowing those who wish to recite prayers (and they are the vast majority of our citizens) to do so, with or without the blessings of the government.

I think the conclusion is inescapable that in the *Engel* decision the Supreme Court in effect gave preference to the dissenters and at the same time violated the establishment clause of the First Amendment by establishing a religion — the religion of secularism.

Public school children are a captive audience. They are compelled to attend school. Their right to the free exercise of religion should not be suspended while they are in attendance. The language of the First Amendment assumes that this basic freedom should be in force at all times and in all places.

Every year at election time the American people are subjected to a lot of pious talk about how government must be made responsive to the needs and wishes of the people. I have a small mountain of correspondence, along with reams of petitions, attesting that the American people *want* the restoration of voluntary prayer to the schools. But to this day it remains an uphill battle to convince a majority of my colleagues of their obligation to rectify the inequity perpetrated by the Supreme Court. I have been reminding them for four years — and I intend to go on reminding them until the free exercise of religion is restored to its full constitutional status.

N. C. CONGRESSIONAL CLUB
P. O. BOX 18848
RALEIGH, NORTH CAROLINA 27609

GENTLEMEN:

☐ I enjoyed Senator Helms' book. Please send me _____ copies for my friends and family. My check is enclosed.

☐ I would also like to receive the North Carolina Congressional Club newsletter, including Senator Helms' news column. Please put me on your mailing list at the address below.

Sincerely,

Name _____

Address _____

City/State _____ Zip _____

CHAPTER TWENTY-TWO

Who's in Charge?

A CONTEMPORARY Christian writer of great eloquence and insight has summarized in one basic question the moral confusion that confronts us today. Simply stated by Malcolm Muggeridge: "Is God in charge of our affairs, or are we?"

He probes the question further: "A great, and growing, body of opinion, some of it ecclesiastical, much of it in worldly terms powerful and influential, takes the view that *we* are now in charge. Whereas formerly it was considered man's highest aim to understand God's purpose for him and his highest achievement to fulfill that purpose, now we are urged to dispense with God altogether, and assume control ourselves of the world, the universe and our own collective and individual destiny. God, we have been told, if He ever existed, has died; as a concept, He is not needed any more. We know enough now about our environment and circumstances, have sufficient control over them to take over. Our apprenticeship is served; mankind has come of age; and the time has come for us to assume command of ourselves and our world in our own right."

Mr. Muggeridge goes on to enumerate the disastrous implications of such a notion. But whenever I have the occasion to ponder his words, I am always struck by how well he has summarized what might be called the fundamental creed of political liberalism.

My work every day throws me into close contact with these very worldly and influential people. When one starts the day with the *Washington Post* or the *New York Times*, then spends hours in committee work, taking testimony and preparing to vote, the current of this thinking sometimes seems overwhelming.

What, I wonder, is to rescue our country from the judgment that is surely and deservedly to come upon us? When I came to the Senate from Raleigh, I had moments of believing that I had only traded my job as a broadcaster for a seat much closer to the great epic tragedy of the West.

But then I began to take the measure of my liberal colleagues and the men whose word literally is law in a hundred diverse bureaucracies. I found in many of them not the calm, self-assurance of people accustomed to having their way. Rather, there was a sense of impending calamity, an awareness that all their great social blueprints were founded on sand. Officials — particularly elected officials — seldom have time to take the measure of their needs. In Washington they work always with one eye over their shoulders, scanning the field for rivals and challengers. The cause of our country has been poorly served by these shallow, vainglorious men whose principles change with every shifting wind.

How different indeed from the stout-hearted souls who established our nation and government! Of the fifty-six men who signed the Declaration of Independence, fourteen lost their lives as captives, soldiers, or casualties of the War for Independence. Many of the signers were brought up in affluence and were unusually well-educated, yet none shrank from putting their lives, their fortunes, and their sacred honor right on the line when they saw the need to do so. One-fourth of them gave up their lives; still others lost their sons; many more saw their lands and property devastated. But to this day their honor remains undiminished.

Why did these heroes take such risks and forfeit the advantages they enjoyed?

The answer is, they did it for *us*. They did it so that we, their posterity, could live in freedom. In doing this, I think they were exemplifying some of the profoundest Christian teachings: the necessity of faith, of sacrifice, and above all, of hope.

I think the lessons of these men should not be looked at, from a twentieth-century point of view, as simply antiquarian lore. The issues they faced then have the most amazing parallels with those facing us today.

The tendency in 1776, as it is today, was toward big government, gun control, swarms of officials presiding over the minutiae of daily life, high taxation, and domestic insurrection. In England, they faced the world's most formidable naval power. There was also, widespread among the people themselves, a desire for peace at any price — even, to quote Patrick Henry, "at the price of chains and slavery."

But Providence raised up men who saw that America had a special destiny in the world. They understood and pursued that destiny, firm in the belief that God would bless their endeavors. That motto — *Annuit Coeptis* — remains to this day on our currency: "He has favored our undertakings."

I believe it is time we printed it not only on our dollar bills, but on our hearts as well. For God *has* blessed our undertakings, and He will continue to do so when we are motivated by a love for freedom under His law. What has supplanted our traditional love of freedom in the meantime is a love of comfort and pleasure and ease. All through the Old Testament we see the panorama of powerful, materialistic nations which crumbled to dust from their obsession with material splendor and personal licentiousness. It certainly wasn't lack of money or power that brought them down.

Today many of our people will go to any lengths to

avoid responsibility. "Give us security, give us mammoth government to superintend our affairs, and we shall be content." The Divine Providence on which our fore-fathers relied has been supplanted by the Providence of the All-Powerful State. I believe that this is the source of deep weakness in America, because it is a transgression of the first and greatest of the Ten Commandments. Again: "Is God in charge of our affairs, or are we?"

Contemporary Americans are the beneficiaries of generations of pioneers who faced unprecedented dangers and hardships, loneliness and isolation to subdue a whole continent and make it fruitful. In this, too, their sacrifices were always borne with the welfare of their children's children firmly in their thinking.

I believe we must now rekindle that concern for the benefit of generations yet to come. Recently we have witnessed a great awakening of interest in preserving the quality of the environment. I believe this should not be limited to physical geography, but should be extended to encompass the political climate our grandchildren live in, and the economic burdens they will have to bear if we squander their precious heritage.

There are those who will argue that such concern is entirely beside the point for us who live in the nuclear age. I think they are mistaken. Of those to whom much has been given, much will be required. Our ancestors continually faced death in many guises, but they never succumbed to great waves of collective despair. We dishonor them when we think that we are the end of the line and proceed to act accordingly.

CHAPTER TWENTY-THREE

Real Strength

As I LOOK back on it, I think it was a little girl's excitement that did it. In any event, I met a most delightful family from western Kentucky one morning several weeks ago, and it was one of those enriching experiences that add a bit of zest to a fellow's day.

They were standing there in the Capitol, just outside the Senate Chamber. I was returning to my office after an eight o'clock meeting, and I heard the little girl exclaim, "Just think, daddy, we're here, we're here!"

Indeed they were, all five of them — daddy and mama; two little girls, eleven and eight respectively; and a little boy named Robbie whom I judged to be about five.

I wish I could describe the excitement of that eleven-year-old, who I later learned is named Myra. She was literally trembling; her eyes were shining; her face was aglow with a genuine, delighted smile.

The family was obviously of modest means. Later I learned that they are a farm family who had been saving their money for more than two years so that they could make a trip to Washington.

I'm not sure what prompted me to intrude — the little girl's excited smile or the fact that I heard her daddy call his son "Robbie." (I have a grandson by the same name, and it's a magic word around our house.)

Anyhow, I did intrude — and as it turned out, it was one of those splendid experiences. Inasmuch as the Senate was not yet in session, I asked Myra if she would like to bring her family into the Senate Chamber.

The empty chamber always seems to me to thunder in its silence. The one hundred highly polished, graceful desks of senators hold place like mute sentinels. Myra walked over, touched one of the desks with her fingertips, and said with that appealing, trembling excitement, "I can't *believe* we're here!"

It was a delightful few minutes that I spent with this wholesome farm family from Kentucky. We visited only briefly, but it was long enough to disclose that here were a man and his wife who love this country and whose children are being taught to love and respect it. And it occurred to me, as I listened to them, that here is the real strength of America: hard-working citizens who understand this nation's basic principles.

In all likelihood, I will never again see these fine people. But in a very real way I am indebted to them for reviving my own spirit. Many times since, when I've walked onto the Senate Floor, I have thought of an eleven-year-old Myra and her excitement. "Just think, daddy, we're here, we're here!"

Myra and her family are the strength of our country. They symbolize the Miracle of America.

CHAPTER TWENTY-FOUR

Conclusion

THE WORLD was in a grim state the day that Saul of Tarsus set out on his journey to Damascus. The known world, in terms of geography as we know it today, was small. *All* of it lay in bondage. There was one government and it was Rome; there was one master and he was Tiberius Caesar.

The centurions made certain that it remained so. There was conformity everywhere, in government and in society. As he pursued his journey, Saul could see the oppression of all who were not friends of Tiberius Caesar. There was the tax gatherer to take the grain from the fields and the flax from the spindles to feed the Roman army and to fill the imperial treasury.

The whole Roman superstate rested on the presumption that man existed to serve Caesar. That was all. Those who thought differently were silenced by the executioner.

Then suddenly a light had come into the world, and a Man from Galilee announced a new message: "Render to Caesar the things that are Caesar's, and to God the things that are God's."

The men of darkness tried to snuff out the light. But the Man from Galilee had warned His followers, "Hurry! Walk while you have the light, lest the darkness overtake you."

These were perilous times involving fateful decisions. Even Saul of Tarsus — now become Paul the apostle — was afraid. He feared that after Tiberius Caesar, there would be other Caesars, and also false prophets, who might convince men that they were nothing more than slaves whose end was this world alone.

Fearing these things, Paul warned that it could come to pass that darkness would again settle over the land, and that men would think only of what they should eat and what they should wear and would give heed only to new Caesars, false prophets, and false promises. It was then that Paul the apostle spoke to his brethren, the Galatians, words that men of all generations would remember:

"Stand fast therefore in the liberty wherewith Christ has made us free, and be not entangled again with the yoke of bondage."

From that time to this, the only guarantor of freedom in the world has been the Christian faith. Only a Christian is secure in his conviction that his soul belongs to God alone. Only a Christian has this defense against the powers of darkness and the ceaseless demands of the secular order.

In many of the same ways that the devil tempts men, he tempts nations as well. Satan did not hesitate to display before the Lord Himself the glittering panorama of the kingdoms of this world in an arrogant act of effrontery and deceit having no equal in the annals of history. The price to be paid for these great kingdoms was nothing less than the worship of Satan. And for his presumption, the Lord delivered Satan a majestic and resounding rebuke.

The devil is still at work today promising the whole panoply of material wealth to those nations that disavow their Christian heritage and accept him as prince of this world. Nation after nation has accepted the devil's bargain, only to find themselves deceived, betrayed, and then destroyed.

Satan has not neglected to tempt America, but for a long time America was immune to his offerings. Until well into this century, our country was dominated by a biblical understanding of life. Our preachers and teachers and judges and families were almost all aware of the sinful nature of man. They recognized the restraints and bounds that God has laid down for man's welfare, and the duty He has laid upon us to work for our daily bread.

In the last quarter-century, however, one by one these theological and moral imperatives have fallen. Too many of our people today act as if there were no God, no Ten Commandments, no prospect of a Day of Judgment — but only material and physical needs that must be satisfied on any terms. The loving and provident God of the Scriptures has been pushed aside in favor of a notion that the civil government is the ultimate provider and lawgiver. There is nothing to distinguish these people fundamentally from the most committed Communists who believe that evil is the consequence, not of sin, but of private property.

Communism has made substantial inroads into the thinking of our people, because it is a counterfeit religion based on the alluring prospect of an abundant life for all. Communism is a perversion of the Christian faith, but to a generation who have no spiritual or moral training, such a disciplined response to human longings looks appealing indeed.

But we have the Word of the Son of God Himself that the Christians, and not the Communists, are called to be the light of the world and the salt of the earth.

This is not an easy calling, because Christ's plan for redeeming the world must be accepted by each individual Christian. Each of us must reform his or her own heart and soul before we can take up the work of helping to regenerate society.

God has given us ample means and abundant grace to use in our work of restoring the rule of His law to our demoralized country. Our first priority in holding back the waves of statism that threaten to engulf us all must be to renew the honor and dignity and prestige of the family. The family has prior right to that of any government.

Almighty God is the author of the family, and the Lord Jesus Himself grew up subject to His human household. Though nothing suits collectivism better than masses of isolated individuals, there can be no just social order which is not based on the Christian concept of the family and the rights pertaining to it.

Many distressed people write to me sorely troubled by their inability to have any impact on the political decisions that are bringing our country closer and closer to collectivism. I try to impress upon these people that the most enduring contribution they can make to our country and to our political system is to work for the security, stability, and welfare of their families. This is the unit that God has ordained as basic to human life and happiness. We must restore and preserve the family as the focus of our personal and social well-being and the strongest defense we have against the totalitarian state.

Each of us has a part to play in bringing about the great spiritual awakening that must come upon this nation before we are brought to our knees by the just chastisements of God. The Old Testament teaches that Israel had a predictable relationship with God. Israel would prosper in the days it lived by the Word of God. Then when it fell away from God's law, through immorality and unbelief, Israel suffered civil strife, inability to maintain peace and security, and finally captivity. But Israel in its affliction would realize the error of its ways and would beseech the Lord to come to the aid of His chosen people. And God would hear His people and would deliver them from their enemies, for He has promised:

> If my people, which are called by my name, shall humble themselves, and pray, and seek my face, and turn from their wicked ways; then will I hear from heaven, and will forgive their sin, and will heal their land.

Christ teaches that God's promise will be honored in New Testament times and peoples. In our country's birth pangs, the officers and men of the Continental Army prayed to God for strength to endure great hardship and prevail over their enemies. God heard them. When the Constitutional Convention was hopelessly deadlocked for weeks in debate, the representatives at last turned to prayer for guidance. God heard them as well, and there emerged one of history's greatest achievements, the Constitution of the United States.

Each of us, then, must place our hope and reliance in God, and in that hope and reliance turn our energies to restoring a government and society that serves us as sons of God. Adroit politicians have successfully divided us into groups of minorities so that now each of us belongs to one minority or another. Thereby our strength is sapped in a disunity designed to keep us in check; a disunity disguised with such utopian slogans as Peace With Honor, Minimum Wage, Racial Equality, Women's Liberation, National Health Insurance, Civil Liberty, and so on and on.

When the shadows of the Gulag Archipelago are looming over the world, we cannot dedicate our energies to any lesser goal than freedom under God's law. We can no longer afford to salve our consciences with the belief that we belong to the stalwart "silent majority." I am indebted to a correspondent who once pointed out to me that the term "silent majority" was coined by the poet Homer eight centuries before Christ. It was the term Homer used to describe the dead.

Our greatest need today — and the greatest need the world had when Saul of Tarsus set out on his journeys — is for us to have faith and courage. These are not dispensed by civil governments or revolutions, but by the Spirit of God.

We need to apply these virtues to every aspect of our lives. But above all, Americans as a people must once again rise up and reclaim their nation from the slothful, divisive, prodigal, and treacherous individuals who have bartered away our freedoms for a mess of pottage.

I call upon all those who feel within themselves the

shackles of despair and unbelief to rise and be about our Father's business as our Lord Jesus Christ gives us the grace to do His work. Like Israel, we must turn to the Author of Liberty to enjoy again what once we had so abundantly.

For additional books, contact the
> Jesse Helms for Senate Committee
> P.O. Box 19433
> Raleigh, North Carolina 27609

1 copy —	$1.75
10 copies —	1.50 each
25 copies —	1.25 each
50 copies —	1.00 each
100 or more —	.75 each